DAY TRADING EASY

A Step-by-Step Guide to Day Trading Strategies e Risk Management

CONTENTS

INTRODUCTION

Success as a day trader will only come to 10% of those who try. It's important to understand why most traders fail so that you can avoid those mistakes. The day traders who lose money in the market are losing because of a failure to either choose the right stocks, manage risk, find proper entries, or follow the rules of a proven strategy. In this book I will teach you trading techniques that I personally use to profit from the market. Before diving into the trading strategies we will first build your foundation for success as a trader by discussing the two most important skills you can possess. I like to say that a day trader is two things, a hunter of volatility and a manager of risk. I'll explain how to find predictable volatility and how to manage your risk so you can make money and be right only 50% of the time. We turn the tables by putting the odds for success in your favor. By picking up this book you show dedication to improve your trading. This by itself sets you apart from the majority of beginner traders.

The act of day trading is simply buying shares of a stock with the intention of selling those shares for a profit, within minutes or hours. In order to profit in such a short window of time, we trade shares of companies that have just released breaking news, made a big earnings announcement or have any type of fundamental catalyst that results in above average interest from retail traders and investors. The type of stocks a day trader will focus on are typically much different from what a long term investor would look for. Day traders acknowledge the high levels of risk associated with trading volatile markets, and they mitigate those risks by holding positions for very short periods of time.

While investors typically look for 5-10% annual returns, day traders look for trades that have the potential to make 5-10% intraday returns. However, in order to profit from intraday moves, most day traders will take large positions which can result in a high level of single stock exposure. Some will even engage in the high risk practice of trading on margin (money borrowed from your broker). For example, a day trader with a $25k trading account may use margin (buying power is 4x the cash balance) and trade as if he had $100k in equity. This is considered leveraging your account. By aggressively trading on margin, if the trader can produce 5% daily returns on the $100k buying power, the trader will grow the $25k initial equity at a rate of 20% per day. The risk of course is that the trader will make a mistake that can cost him everything. Unfortunately, this is the fate for 9 out of 10 traders. The cause of these career ending mistakes result from a failure to manage risk.

Imagine a trader who has just taken 9 successful trades. In each trade there was a $50 risk and $100 profit potential. This means each trade had the potential to double the risk for a 2:1 profit loss ratio. The first 9 successful trades produce $900 in profit. On the 10th trade, when the position is down $50, instead of accepting the loss, the untrained trader purchases more shares at a lower price to reduce his cost basis. Once he is down $100, he continues to hold and is unsure of whether to hold or sell. The trader finally takes the loss when he is down $1k. This is a trader who has a 90% success rate, but is still a losing trader because he failed to manage his risk. We will discuss in detail how to identify stocks and find good trade opportunities, but first we will focus on developing your understanding of risk management. Traders that don't utilize risk management techniques stand a good chance of being among the 90% of retail traders who lose money in the market.

Over my years as a trader and as a trading coach, I have worked with thousands of students. The majority of those students experienced a devastating loss at some point due to avoidable mistakes. It is easy to understand how a trader can fall into the position of a margin call (a debt to your broker). The money to trade on margin is easily available, and the allure of quick profits can lead both new and seasoned traders to ignore commonly accepted rules of risk management. The 10% of traders who consistently profit from the market share one common skill. They cap their losses. They accept that each trade has a predetermined level of risk and they adhere to the rules they set for that trade. This is part of a well-defined trading strategy. It's common for an untrained trader to adjust their risk parameters mid-trade to accommodate a losing position. For instance, if they said their stop loss is at -$50, and the trade goes down to -$60, they might say they'll hold for just a few more minutes to see if it comes back up. Before you know it, they are looking at an $80-100 loss, or worse, and they are wondering how it happened. I'll admit that it's extremely difficult to achieve the level of discipline to sell when you hit your max loss on a trade. Nobody wants to lose, but the best traders are great losers. They accept their losses with grace and move on to the next trade. They never allow one trade the ability to destroy their account or their career. This characteristic will keep them in business as a day trader for a long time.

The skill to take losses and not allow them to cause you to lose focus is an act of mindfulness. Our human emotions often work against us while we are in trades. The emotions of fear and greed are present in every trader. The successful traders are able to experience those emotions without acting on them. When you allow emotions to overtake your rational thought process, you run the risk of over trading, exposing yourself to unnecessary risk, and unplanned losses. It takes years of emotional conditioning to be able to sit for eight hours watching the computer screens while maintaining composure the whole time. For new traders, we encourage starting with shorter blocks of time and maintaining a constant focus on the idea of thinking like a risk manager.

Buying Long or Selling Short

If you are new to trading you may not be familiar with the concept of selling short. Traders who sell short are borrowing shares from their broker to sell those shares at a high price, with the intention of buying the shares back at a lower price, and profiting from the drop. When you sell short, your account will show in your open positions window, a negative position (e.g. -1000 shares). You have borrowed 1000 shares from your broker and sold them. The broker expects that you will buy back those shares. When you buy back those shares, it is called covering your position. Some traders have a short bias and prefer to trade as stocks drop. One of the risks with short selling is that if the stock goes up, you will eventually be forced to cover your position. Since theoretically prices can climb infinitely, a trader could experience an infinite loss if they do not cover their open short position.

Conversely, when you buy stock to the long side, your maximum loss is capped to the amount of shares you purchased. The worst case scenario is the stock goes to $0. With a short position, if you short 1000 shares of a stock at $5.00, and it goes up to $100.00, your $5k position becomes a $95k loss. Throughout this book, we will discuss examples of momentum trades that involve buying stock to the long side, but these patterns could be equally applied to the inverse pattern in order to short stocks.

Whether you are a short seller or a long biased trader, it is important to know about the Short Sale Restriction (SSR). This was designed to reduce downward volatility and help prevent potential stock crashes. When Short Sale Restriction has been activated on a stock, you can only short the stock when the price is moving up. This prevents people fueling a crash by shorting as the price is dropping. SSR is turned on when a stock drops more than 10% in price versus the previous days close. The SSR is an example of an indicator that tells us the markets have a built in bias for trading to the long side. There is no such thing as a long buy restriction. A stock can surge up 100% and you can continue to buy as it surges. This is one of the reasons I prefer to be a long biased trader.

It's also important to note that shorting is not available for all stocks. The ability to short a stock requires your broker to have shares available to borrow. If they have a small inventory, you may not be able to short that stock.

What you will learn

If you have tried day trading or watched somebody else day trade, you already know the concepts are simple, but being successful at day trading is like walking a tightrope. If you watch somebody doing it they make it look easy, but when you try it, it seems nearly impossible. This is the experience most new day traders will go through. In fact, it's the same experience I went through when I was learning to trade. I have found that the best trades are the ones that have the most obvious setups and start to work in our favor almost immediately. If I find myself in the position of holding trades that aren't performing or I start trying to force trades to work under less than ideal setups, I usually get into trouble. I'd encourage traders to focus on the obvious setups we teach rather than overcomplicating things.

In this book we will teach you the fundamental concepts required for day trading. You will learn how to manage risk, how to choose stocks worth trading, how to identify potential setups, how to enter and exit trades, and how to manage your emotions while you are trading. By taking the time to educate yourself, you are already proving a willingness to learn, and that puts you ahead of the majority of new traders. Most new traders will trade unproven strategies and then wonder why they are losing money. While you are in training, it is important that you only trade in a simulated account. You have to practice the strategies we teach and work on building your skills before ever trading in a live account. In our live trading courses, we review the performance of all our students to ensure they are meeting the metrics and statistics of a profitable trader. This means we evaluate accuracy rates, average losses versus average winners, how much risk they take in their trades and how they behave under stress of difficult markets or losing positions. Once students have proven they can be profitable in a simulated environment, they will be ready to switch to live trading with strict size and risk restrictions. Students in our live day trading chat room benefit from being able to trade side by side with me, and hundreds of other professional traders. We have trained the students in our community to be the best possible traders, thus increasing the overall skill of our trading group.

CHAPTER 1

If you are considering a career as a day trader, you cannot ignore the statistics that show only 1 in 10 traders will be able to make a living at it. I am not saying this to discourage you from trading. We are going to talk about the reasons why most traders fail so you can avoid making those same mistakes. I believe failure is an option, one that is often chosen without the trader realizing it. Just as failure is an option, so is success, if you make the right decisions. Most traders that I have seen fail were unable to follow simple rules of risk management. We will be discussing the rules of risk management in the next chapter, but let us first talk about the reason why it is so difficult to follow the rules. Trading becomes extremely emotional when we are faced with losses and even wins. Being a day trader puts you in the unique position of having to experience a financial loss every single day. On a good day, you will win more than you lose and end the day with a net profit. But, even on the best days there will still typically be at least a few losing trades. There is no such thing as a strategy or a trader who is 100% successful on every trade they take. The best traders may be profitable every month out of the year, but it would be unreasonable and statistically improbable to expect 100% accuracy. Even investors who make billions of dollars have losing investments. This means you will have to face loss and become comfortable with it. The traders I have known who have failed were never able to cope with loss. They allowed the fear of loss to guide their trading decisions.

The hunt for the Holy Grail

If you are a trader who is constantly jumping from strategy to strategy or technical indicator to technical indicator, you may be suffering from the Holy Grail syndrome. These traders will spend tremendous amounts of time and energy searching for the perfect combination of indicators and strategies that will always give them winning trades. On the surface, it makes sense to search for the best strategy, but that's not the motivation of these traders. Just below the surface is a deep fear of loss. It is a fear so strong that it motivates these traders to search endlessly for that perfect strategy in hopes of preventing them from having to experience any more losses. These traders sometimes work to create automated trading systems, search out other traders they can mirror trade (following trade for trade), or simply jump from strategy to strategy until they have exhausted their financial resources and give up. If you are in the group of traders hunting for the Holy Grail, I would encourage you to read this carefully: you can lose 50% of the time and still make money just as easily as you can be right 90% of the time and still lose money. You have to focus not on your percentage of success, but on your profit loss ratios.

Profit Loss Ratios

Profit loss ratios are often overlooked by novice traders. We have our students trading with a minimum 2:1 profit loss ratio (every trade has the profit potential of 2x the risk). With a 2:1 profit loss ratio, our students can make money and be profitable with only 50% success rate. When I work with students, the first thing I look at is their trade history. I want to know their profit loss ratios and their average percentage of success. These numbers will tell me if they have a sustainable strategy. If you can trade with a 2:1 profit loss ratio, it becomes much easier for you to succeed. Most traders who fail will be trading with negative profit loss ratios. Meaning they lose more on average than they win. Regardless of their percentage of success, they will have set the bar so high, it becomes almost impossible to succeed. The odds are stacked against them. From a purely statistical standpoint, a negative profit loss ratio of 1:2 (you lose 2x what you win on average) is an unsustainable strategy unless you maintain 75% success rate. After years of trading, I can assure you that maintaining a 75% success is not easy. Often times the failed traders will exit the market having never realized they were destined for failure because they did not learn about the profit loss ratios required in order to be profitable.

Profit Loss Ratio Statistics

2:1 Profit Loss Ratio = 33% is your Break Even before commissions

1:1 Profit Loss Ratio = 50% is your Break Even before commissions

1:2 Profit Loss Ratio = 66% is your Break Even before commissions

Fear of Loss in Trading

Fear is a natural emotion, but it's difficult when your job requires you to experience fear on a regular basis. Many traders will experience fear in a number of ways. The most obvious is the fear of financial loss. We acknowledge that investing in the market and day trading in particular is high risk, but when we are faced with the decision to take a trade and expose ourselves to a potential loss, fear can begin to guide our decisions. A less obvious form of fear is the fear of missing a big move in the markets. If you suddenly see a stock start to jump up on what might appear to be breaking news, or you see a reversal begin to take shape, you may feel inclined to jump into the market out of fear of missing a potential winner. The fear has guided your decision and led you into an unplanned trade. You may have purchased at a price too far away from your stop or taken more shares than your risk tolerance allows. In a split second you made a decision and broke your rules. The result when these trades go badly will be a larger loss than your strategy and rules allow for. When I speak with a trader about a massive loss, they often say "it happened so fast." They made a quick decision and it was the wrong decision. In reviewing my own trading performance, my biggest losses were spontaneous trades I jumped into on an impulse. I see the markets starting to move and jump into a stock without fully analyzing my risk. Unfortunately, when emotions are guiding a trader's decisions, big mistakes are common. We will discuss techniques for managing emotions while trading, but first let's review a few other examples of erratic trading brought on by emotions.

Holding Losers Too Long

As you can see, our fear of loss in trading can manifest itself in some unusual and outright counterproductive ways. Many beginner traders and most failed traders will experience the tendency to hold their losers too long and sell their winners too soon. The driving emotion that leads to this behavior is a fear of loss. Why does a trader hold losers too long? It is because a trade is not a loss until you have hit the sell button. There is always the chance that the price could pop back up until you hit the sell button. The fear of making the loss real keeps you in the trade because it makes you think about finding a way to turn the trade around instead of just taking the loss and moving on to a different trade. The reality is that small losses are not a big deal, but a trader in an emotional state does not think that way. Sometimes traders will make a bad trade worse by averaging down, adding shares at a lower price to reduce their cost basis. This typically results in bigger losses when it is not part of a proven strategy that involves scaling in and out of trades by averaging. I have worked with traders who set $200 max losses, and on a trade when they were down $200, instead of simply cutting the loss, they decided to add more shares so they could trade out of the loss. These trades would often end in losses of -$1000 or more. In hindsight, it is easy to say the right thing to do was simply cut the loss at -$200 and follow the rules you made for yourself. Unfortunately, in the heat of the moment, emotions take control and your rational thought processes get thrown out the window. In those cases, the fear of loss actually resulted in the trader taking bigger losses than the rules of trading would allow for. This is the exact opposite of what you want! The most important skill for a new trader to understand and adopt is the ability to cap their losses.

Selling Winners Too Soon

If you enter a trade that had a good profit potential and it fit into your trading strategy, the last thing you want to do is sell the trade before it has had a chance to work. If you are up 10 cents on a trade that has the potential to make 50 cents, there is no reason to sell it. Why do so many traders sell their winners too soon? It is because the fear of loss has guided their decisions. It is the fear of the small winner turning into a loser that convinces us to sell the trade too soon. Just as a loser isn't real until you hit the sell button, a winner isn't real until you've hit the sell button and locked it up. In the short term we feel happy to have locked up some profit, even if only a small one, but the big picture is that you are forming a habit of capping your winners. To be a successful trader you have to cap your losers and let your winners run. You will want that occasional big winner, because those will tide you over during periods of slow trading. A trader that sells winners too soon and holds losers too long has the habits of a failing trader. To avoid failure these traders must address how their emotions are influencing their trading. Instead of selling the full position when sitting on a small profit, I combat that urge by selling a partial position and adjusting my stop. This means I will walk away with a small profit (not a loss), but still have a position in the trade to let it realize its full potential. This is called scaling out. Scaling out is a great trade management method of keeping partial positions with a good cost average. To maintain discipline, I refuse to sell my final position until I get stopped out by a valid exit indicator.

Embrace Loss as a Part of the Business

Instead trying to search for the Holy Grail, or give in to the urge to hold losers and sell winners, we must simply accept loss as part of the business of day trading. We cannot fight it. Every day trader will experience losses. Becoming a good day trader means being a good loser. The trick to being a good loser is learning to cap your losses at a set dollar amount and sticking with it. The hard part is holding yourself to the rules. Day trading requires a tremendous amount of discipline and self-control. It is a job that will challenge you in more ways than you would imagine. In the example of the trader with a 90% success rate that was still losing money, he failed to cap his losses. Being that type of trader is a choice. By teaching you about profit loss ratios and the importance of capping your loses, we are empowering you to make the choice to be a successful trader.

Discipline as a Practice

In our trading courses, we spend a great deal of time working with students to help them improve their discipline. Many of our students found us after taking other trading courses and finding themselves still stuck in a cycle of poor trading habits, trading losses, and disappointment. We realized that textbook concepts of trading, which are important and will be covered later on, are not enough. Understanding fundamental concepts of trading on their own are not enough to be a successful trader. You must also think and act like a successful trader. This means selling losers quickly and holding partial positions in your winners as long as possible. In order to help our students improve their ability to be disciplined, we require a min of 30 minutes of exercise and 15 minutes of meditation every day. I use exercise and meditation to help train my mind to cope with stress. By forcing myself to do these two things every day, I am practicing discipline. In the moment when I am in a trade and need to make a hard decision, I need to be able to fight the urge to sell the winners too soon and hold the losers too long. By practicing discipline in others areas of our life, we strengthen that muscle memory and improve our ability to maintain composure while trading. Practicing discipline is a way of conditioning our minds to become accustomed to a feeling of discomfort. Rather than taking steps to alleviate the feeling, we can train ourselves to withstand it. When we sell a winner too soon or hold a loser too long, we are allowing the uncomfortable emotion of fear to guide our decision. Most of the successful traders I know have strict exercise regimens because it helps improve their trading performance. We know it is impossible to block out the emotions such as fear, they will still surface within every trader. However, the difference between winning traders and losing traders is that winning traders will not subject their strategy to the emotion. They recognize the emotion and allow it to exist without acting on those feelings. This is a critical step in the emotional development of any trader. I would encourage you to begin journaling your emotions while trading. The first step to changing your behavior is becoming aware of your emotional patterns and their impact on your trading performance. As we discussed earlier, you can have a deep understanding of all the textbook concepts of trading, but still fail to succeed because you have not achieved the emotional training to be a trader. We focus on providing our students with a well-rounded education that includes both textbook and emotional development.

It is important to remember that discipline is not like learning to ride a bike or learning to swim. Discipline is very much like a muscle that can be strengthened when exercised or atrophy when ignored. Even after years of trading, I still find myself occasionally giving in to my instinct to chase a stock for fear of missing the move, to sell a winner too soon, or hold a loser a little too long. Every day when I trade I have to fight against my natural instincts. Unfortunately many of our natural human instincts do not encourage healthy trading patterns. If I had to guess I would say almost all successful traders have spent thousands of hours training their minds to fight against counterproductive impulses. I am sure there are some traders that have a natural aptitude for the mindset required to be profitable, but I believe the majority of us have to really work at it. It took me years to become successful, and looking back I have realized it was because of the emotional obstacles that stood in my way. I had a great concept of stocks, chart patterns, basic strategies, but I kept falling into the cycle of big losers and small winners. It took a long time before I developed the self-awareness to realize what was causing those actions. My hope is that by reading this, you will avoid the years of trial and error it took me to learn these important lessons.

CHAPTER 2

RISK MANAGEMENT

One of the first things I told you was that day traders are hunters of volume and managers of risk. In this chapter we are going to discuss risk management. As an aspiring day trader, you already understand that day trading is one of the riskiest investment techniques. The reason traders choose to day trade instead of make more traditional, longer term investments is because day trading can produce much larger gains in a faster time frame. Day trading is one of the fastest ways to grow a small account, when it is done properly. The problem is most people will not trade properly. Successful traders can utilize $25k accounts to produce over $50k per year, or 200% in returns. It would not be realistic, however, for a trader to utilize a $250 million account to produce $500 million per year. The markets typically do not have the liquidity to support a trader entering or exiting a multi-million dollar position within minutes, but positions of tens of thousands or even hundreds of thousands of dollars can be executed almost immediately. This allows day traders with accounts under $1 million and as low as $25,000, to utilize leverage and high speed trading techniques to produce large percentage gains. When a trader reaches a point where they are managing more money than they can efficiently day trade, they would typically begin to branch out by adding longer term investments to diversify the portfolio.

While understanding that day trading is one of the highest risk trading techniques, the potential for a big reward captures our interest. We can acknowledge that within the realm of day trading, there will be relatively higher risk day trading strategies and relatively lower risk day trading strategies. Our goal is to develop a trading strategy to maximize profit potential while taking steps to minimize risk. Every time you take a trade, you must evaluate the risk of the trade and weigh that against the reward. Often times our judgment can be clouded by our emotional state or previous trading experiences. If we recently experienced a loss, we may decide to take more risk on the next trade to compensate for the previous loss. Or a more conservative trader may decide to reduce position sizes or even skip good trade opportunities because the last time they traded that setup they lost money. It takes a heightened level of self-awareness to recognize when we are making clear risk reward decisions and when our judgment is clouded. This is a skill that is learned over time. You can develop a sense of mindfulness by journaling while you trade and then reviewing your notes after the market closes.

Different Types of Risk

When we talk about risk there are a few different types of risk you need to understand. As day traders we are primarily concerned about the distance between our entry and our stop (the price where we will sell for a loss). Your stop loss should be based on a recent support or resistance area on the chart and should always fall within your maximum dollar loss amount. The majority of losses we experience will be when a trade drops down and hits the stop price.

The second type of risk we have to be mindful of is the volatility in the market. As day traders we love volatility, but it also presents a risk because extremely volatile markets can result in larger losses than we may have originally planned for. Since we know that there is a spectrum of risk in day trading, we choose to avoid day trading during moments of unpredictable volatility, such as breaking news. When news is realized, individual stocks or the market at large can trade in a very wide and volatile range. Instead of jumping into the market during that peak in volatility, we wait for the dust to settle before determining a potential trade opportunity.

The third type of risk is your exposure risk. Exposure is calculated by multiplying the share price by the number of shares you are holding. As an investor, you have to factor in exposure risk since positions are held for a long time. An investor typically will not allocate more than 10% of the portfolio to any single stock. In contrast, day traders who use leverage may experience particularly high levels of exposure risk. While this level of risk has to be carefully monitored, most day traders are able to mitigate that risk by holding shares for short periods of time.

Stock Halts

A type of risk that can be a nightmare for day traders using large positions are stock halts. Trading can be halted by the exchanges at any time. There are a number of different types of stock halts. There are market wide stock halts which only occur when there is a technical glitch or some type of computer errors in the exchange. These halts can last for a few minutes, hours or potentially longer. These are rare. The more common stock halts are volatility halts and halts pending the release of material news. Anytime a stock is halted, it can reopen at a much different price. The risk is that a stock could reopen far below your maximum loss amount. We can take certain steps to avoid halts by understanding what causes halts. The market has created what are called circuit breaker halts. If a stock rises or falls more than 10% in a 5min period, the stock can be halted for five minutes. This is a volatility pause to give traders a chance to get their bearings, analyze news, and slow down. This is a measure to prevent flash crash situations. In volatile markets, these types of halts can be fairly common. Often times if some type of news about the company is leaked it can result in a rapid move and then a volatility halt. When stocks are halted going up, they often open higher. Conversely, when they are halted going down, they often open lower. When stocks are halted pending news, it means the company is releasing significant, material news. Once the news has been released, the stock will be scheduled to reopen. If the news is bad, the stock can open significantly lower. This is one of the greatest risks in trading. Stocks susceptible to being halted pending news include stocks surging up rapidly for no apparent reason. In these cases it is not uncommon for the company to issue a statement regarding the price action, or to address the rumors that may be causing the price action. Although stocks can be halted at any time pending news, news is typically released when the market is closed.

Another type of stock halt which is common with penny stocks, but not as common with higher priced stocks is a halt pending government investigation. This is typically the result of a stock being used for market manipulation and fraud. Stocks halted pending an investigation can remain halted for weeks or even months.

As day traders, we have to be mindful of the potential for stock halts and limit our positions on stocks that are at risk for being halted. High risk stocks include penny stock companies and stocks trading on unconfirmed news that has not been released by the company itself. Despite our best efforts to avoid being caught in a halt, it can happen. This is one of the reasons trading on margin can be so dangerous. In the event you are caught in a halt and the stock reopens down 20%, if you were trading on margin, it could result in a massive loss or even a margin call from your broker.

A Day Traders Statistical Advantage (2:1 Profit Loss Ratios)

When I was a new trader, I would take extremely large positions without any real understanding of the level of risk I was taking. I would enter trades without a predetermined max loss, and if the trade went against me, I would become paralyzed by fear. I would be unable to think or make a decision as I would watch the loss get bigger and bigger. The first mistake was entering a trade without first outlining the risk versus the reward. As an example, I would often buy stocks as they approached whole dollar levels. So I might buy 1000 shares of a stock at $8.90 with the target of selling it at $9.10 for 20 cents profit. Unfortunately, when the stock would pullback, I would often hold until it broke below the nearest half dollar of $8.50. In this example, I would be risking 40 cents to make 20 cents. This is a negative profit loss ratio which requires a 66% accuracy rate in order to break even before commissions. This is not a sustainable ratio, especially for a new trader. When I was a new trader I did not know anything about profit loss ratios, and I continued to make these uneducated trades and then wonder why I was losing money. Using a 2:1 profit loss ratio, my proper stop on that trade should have been $8.80 instead of $8.50. With a 10 cent stop and a 20 cent profit target, I could justify taking that trade. That means my proper stop was only 25% of the loss I was taking as an untrained trader. That's a huge difference! This meant that by using proper risk management, I could potentially reduce my losses on those types of trades by over 75%. It is extremely important to understand, regardless of your strategy or the setups you trade, that every trade has the potential to double what you are risking. If you do not have the potential to win twice as much you risk, you should not be taking the trade. By simply understanding profit loss ratios and the huge statistical advantage of a 2:1 profit loss ratio, you have set yourself ahead of the majority of new traders.

Data Mine Your Trade History

If you are not already tracking all of your trades in an excel document, I suggest you start doing this now. The information you want to track is the type of setup, time, symbol, price, entry, exit, amount made, amount lost and notes. I have been tracking all of my trades for years and have the benefit of thousands and thousands of trades available for review. I can sort my data based on the strategy, the profits or losses, or the time of day. I dig into the analytics of my trading performance to get a deeper understanding of where I have strengths and where I need to make adjustments. If for example you recognize that the majority of your profits are in the morning, and your biggest losses are in the afternoon, you can begin to become more mindful during afternoon trading. You can also keep track of your profit loss ratios on a monthly basis and always work to improve your statistics. If you trade 500,000 shares per month and you can improve your average profits by 1 cent per share, it will increase your profits by $5,000 per month. This shows you that very small adjustments in your statistics can result in huge differences at the end of the month. This also highlights the tightrope traders must walk. The difference between success and failure can be the matter of a slight adjustment in your ratios. The part of your profit loss ratio that is easiest to control is your max loss.

Capping your Losses - Be good at being wrong

When I speak with a trader who recently experienced a large loss, I like to spend time reviewing the trade that resulted in the loss. I always begin by asking the trader what their risk was when they entered the trade. Rarely does a beginner trader enter a position intending to risk as much as they ultimately lose. That is the first mistake. Every time we take a trade, we must know how much we are risking. This means understanding the logical place to sell the stock for a loss if the trend or the setup fails. Before getting into the chart patterns and the definitions of exit indicators, we will first say that we stop out of all trades when they hit our max loss. Unfortunately, many traders enter position without a max loss in mind.

Every trading plan should have a max loss per trade and a max loss per day. We recommend students set their daily max loss at their daily profit target. When they have a $200 daily profit target, if they are down $200 on the day they shut down their computer and walk away.

Although it is difficult to accept defeat, it is far more important to realize that once you have exceeded your max loss, your judgment is almost guaranteed to become compromised. It is always best to walk away instead of attempting to trade in a compromised emotional state. Just as we have a max loss per day, we also have a max loss per trade. I typically set my max loss at about 25% of my daily goal. If I take a trade and the market suddenly turns against me, I take the loss. Over the years of working with students, I have found that some students are very good at taking their losses, while others struggle to press the sell button. Some even turn short term day trades into long swing trades. If you are in the group of traders who frequently find themselves down beyond your pre-determined max loss, I would consider setting automatic stop orders with your broker. If the price falls below the stop price, your order will automatically execute and you avoid having to press the sell button yourself. Even though it can be difficult to hand over this aspect of trade management to the computer, it is sometimes the best technique for students who struggle to take the losses early. When you are trading, it is important to remind yourself that regardless of how you traded last week or last month, today is your opportunity to prove to yourself that you can follow rules and stick to your trading plan. If you want to succeed as a trader, it is paramount that you are able to hold yourself to the rules of max loss per trade and max loss per day. Ultimately, this means walking away from the computer when you hit your max loss for the day, even if it is difficult.

Day trading is a career where you can make a catastrophic mistake, and then keep trading moments later. You could take a 30,000 share position, lose $15,000, and then do it again five more times in a row. In just one day and a handful of trades, you could easily blow up your entire account. This type of event is the result of emotionally fueled trading. By forcing yourself to walk away after hitting your max loss, you can avoid the temptation to fall into a cycle of increasing your risk and trying to make back your losses. In other careers, race car driving for instance, if you crash your car into the wall you are done with the race and have to wait until the next race. The very nature of that type of job gives you a period of time to reflect on the mistakes you made that resulted in the accident. Day trading does not come with these built-in time out periods after we make a mistake. We have to build them into our trading plan because they are extremely important for our emotional development as a trader. They are what prevent us from making mistakes when we are in a heightened emotional state.

Balancing your Risk

If you take 10 trades in a day, and you risk $100 on the first nine trades and then risk $1,000 on the 10th trade, it doesn't matter if you have a 90% success rate when you lose on the last trade. You will be a losing trader. This is an element of risk management called balancing risk. You never want to have one trade weighted so heavily with risk that it has the power to erase previous winners. Even if the final trade had the 2:1 profit loss potential (risking $1,000 to make $2,000), it is a poor decision because the risk of that one trade far outweighs your average risk per trade. Many traders, including myself, will adjust our risk per trade throughout the day based on our performance and to adapt to greater market conditions. This is a common practice used to increase profits on days when trading is good and reduce losses on days when trading is difficult. The difference is that I am adjusting risk in smaller increments, so the impacts of winners or losers will not have a strong effect on my overall performance. If I risk $100 on the first six trades, I may decide to increase risk to $150 or decrease risk to $75 on seventh, but I would not make a drastic change to my risk parameters in the middle of a trading day. Many beginner traders will have a great day until they decide to swing for the fences and take a high risk position on what they think is a perfect setup. If they lose on that high risk trade, they will give back their entire profits from the day and potentially go into the red. This is a disappointing financial loss, but what is even worse is the loss of confidence and the impact that it has on your emotions. This is the type of behavior that can quickly cause a trader to fall into a cycle of emotionally fueled trading known as revenge trading. Trying to quickly make back the losses by taking increasingly risky trades. To avoid this situation entirely, a trader must balance their risk across all trades, so if that final trade is a loser, it does not ruin their day or their psychological control over future trades.

Gamblers think about Profits, Traders think about Risk

The stock market is a place where all different personalities come together to trade. You will find long term investors, institutional investors, activist investors, retail traders, and you will also find gamblers. Unfortunately, day trading has a negative connotation to some who consider it the equivalent to gambling. Any full-time trader understands that that is far from reality. A trader makes decisions based on a strategy that has historical data to support it. The only way to make a career out of trading is to understand your risk on every trade and to follow the rules of your trading plan. But, there will always be those who simply gamble with their trading accounts by taking reckless positions in the search of huge profits. If you want to gamble, you might as well go to a casino. The odds of having a lucky trade and making a fortune in the stock market are extremely slim. You cannot base your strategy or your career on luck. Greed is a powerful emotion that, a lot like fear, can allow you to throw out your rational thought processes. If you ever find yourself feeling that emotion of greed kicking in, it is a good time to turn off your platform and walk away. Since we are trading with and against the best traders in the world, if we are not able to trade at our peak performance levels, we should not be trading.

Add to Winners not to Losers

Although there are many traders and investors that utilize a strategy of scaling in, adding shares at various prices to get a good cost basis, I avoid adding to stocks that are below my entry price for day trades. If I purchase a stock at $10.00 and it drops to $9.50, I could double my position and adjust my cost basis to $9.75, but then I am adding to a losing position. If it drops to $9.25, I will experience a loss double than the initial loss if I had simply sold at $9.50. In all my years of trading, I have found the best trades work almost immediately. Occasionally, I will get into a trade and it will nearly touch my stop and then turn around and end up being a winner, but more often, those trades turn into losers. Instead of adding to a losing trade, I prefer to cut the loss and move on to the next opportunity. When you focus on adding to losers, you risk making the loss bigger and you miss the opportunity to find a better setup.

In contrast, if I buy a stock at $10.00 and it goes up to $10.50, I may double my position and have a new cost basis of $10.25. If the stock surges up to $10.75 or $11.00 I'll make more with the increased position, and if it the stock drops back down to $10.25 or $10.00, I can sell for breakeven or for a small loss. Adding to winning trades gives you the potential to have big winners, while adding to losers gives you the potential for big losses. Since we want to focus on capping our losses, we need to avoid adding to losers.

Stock Picking versus Risk Management

This is a good time to remind you that you can be a profitable trader with an accuracy rate of 50% or less, as long as you have a good profit loss ratio. Being profitable is not about being right on every trade, it's about capping your losses and taking trades that provide the opportunity for winners that will exceed the losers. Early on I made the example of the trader who loses money despite a 90% success rate. This trader may be a great stock picker, but his lack of risk management results in a losing strategy. Picking good stocks is important, but clearly it is not as important as managing your risk on every trade. I say this to remind you to focus first and foremost on your risk and your max loss on each trade. In the next chapter, we will discuss stock selection as an extension of risk management. By trading the right stocks, we can improve our likelihood for success especially when we combine risk management techniques.

CHAPTER 3

STOCK SELECTION - CHOOSING THE RIGHT STOCKS TO TRADE

In the last chapter we talked about the importance of risk management. We will continue to touch back on the theme of risk management and emotional conditioning throughout this chapter. By trading only the strongest stocks and applying the principles of good risk management, we can give ourselves a huge statistical advantage for success. There are thousands of stocks available to trade each day, but only a few that are actually good candidates for day trading. There are so many that a new trader can quickly become overwhelmed. Often, new traders refer to a watch list of companies they are familiar with. While this may be suitable for some longer term investment strategies, it is not appropriate for day trading. For day trading, there are usually only a small handful of stocks each day that I would consider the right stocks to trade. We have a very specific list of requirements for what makes a stock worth trading on any given day. Most day traders will trade hundreds of different stocks each month, rarely trading the same stocks for more than a few days at a time. The reason we trade so many different stocks is because we are only interested in stocks with volatility and heavy trading volume. Stocks trade on heavy volume because they have a high level of retail interest. High levels of retail interest are typically driven by news, but are sometimes driven by stocks trading at extreme highs or lows. If you look at almost any chart, you will see a few days where the stock traded on extremely high relative volume. Those days are often accompanied by a big gap on the chart. Those are the days we would be most interested in trading that stock. I often remind our students that on any given day, there is a stock having a once in a year event. As a day trader, we have to be willing to jump from stock to stock in order to find the type of price action that can result in at least 5-10% intraday moves.

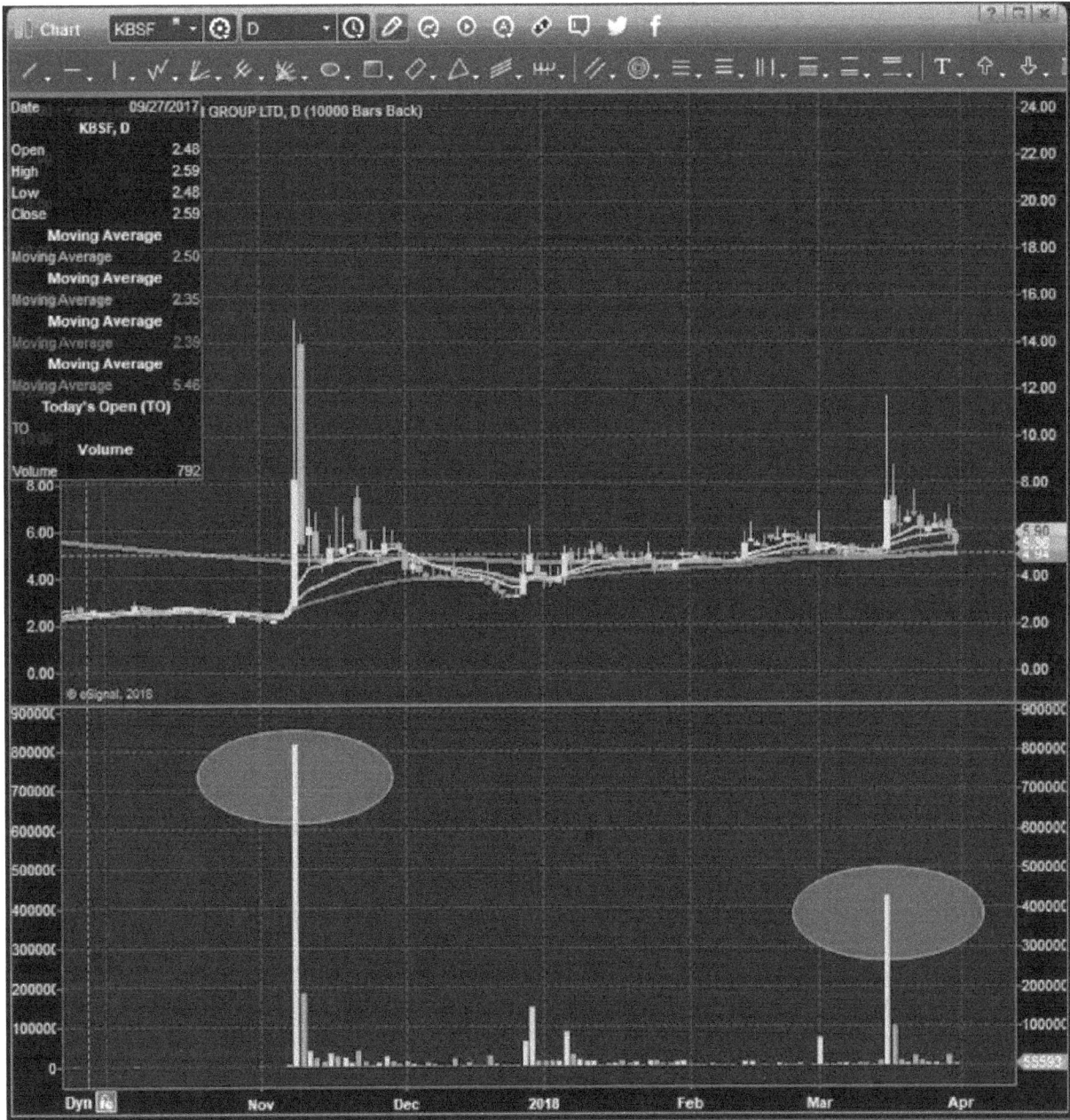

Chart of a stock showing the days with big volume. Those were

the days this was a stock in play for day traders.

Stocks must have Volume

As day traders, we look for stocks that are trading on above average volume. On any given day, algorithmic trading computers account for more than half of the volume in the market. If we see a stock that is trading on below average volume, it is safe to assume that day traders have very little interest in that stock and that the majority of the volume is controlled by high frequency trading computers. These trading computers will buy and sell shares which will result in volume and chart patterns. The problem for day traders is, that when we look at these charts and recognize a familiar pattern, we can be fooled into thinking it is a good buying opportunity. A good looking setup is never complete without above average volume. We need above average volume to confirm that thousands of other traders are watching this same chart. When we are watching a setup forming and we expect a breakout to the upside, that breakout is the result of thousands of traders all buying up shares. In fact, we are one of those buyers! That means as day traders we should only trade stocks other people are trading.

There are a few techniques for making sure we are trading the right stocks. The most obvious technique is to simply look at the daily volume. If a stock trades an average of 500k shares per day and has already traded 2 million shares, there is above average interest. The other option is to use stock scanning software to scan for stocks with high relative volume. The relative volume for the day is translated into a number, a ratio. '1' is average and '2' being 2x average. Stocks can trade on any multiple of relative volume, so anything above a '2' is interesting.

The Hunt for a Catalyst

Every morning starts the same way for me. I look at the stocks trading on heavy volume in the pre-market session. This is often an indicator of early retail interest that will carry over into the trading day. I review each of the stocks trading on high volume to see if there is a catalyst. A biotech or pharmaceutical stock that has just released results from a clinical study could be interesting, or a stock that just reported a big earnings release would be worth watching. I don't put a tremendous amount of energy into researching the catalyst beyond confirming there is a reason that the stock is moving up or down. Even the best news releases sometimes result in poor price action, so I remind myself to always follow the chart and not the fundamentals of the catalyst. Investors focus on fundamentals, but traders focus on chart patterns and technical analysis. We have to remember that we are traders and keep our attention on the chart patterns at all times.

When I'm reviewing pre-market leaders, it is important to check for buy outs. When a stock has been bought out overnight it will trade the next morning at the new price, and typically there will be a huge amount of volume as people buy and sell shares they have been holding. The problem is that since the stock has been bought out, the value of the stock has been determined. If a buyout is priced at 4.00 for example, the stock will trade almost exactly at 4.00 all day long. There is no reason to short the stock or buy the stock knowing the value of the company has become fixed at 4.00. The reason these stocks trade on high relative volume is because long term investors sell their positions at the buyout price. Anytime we see a buy out on the gap scanner we disregard it and move on to the next stock.

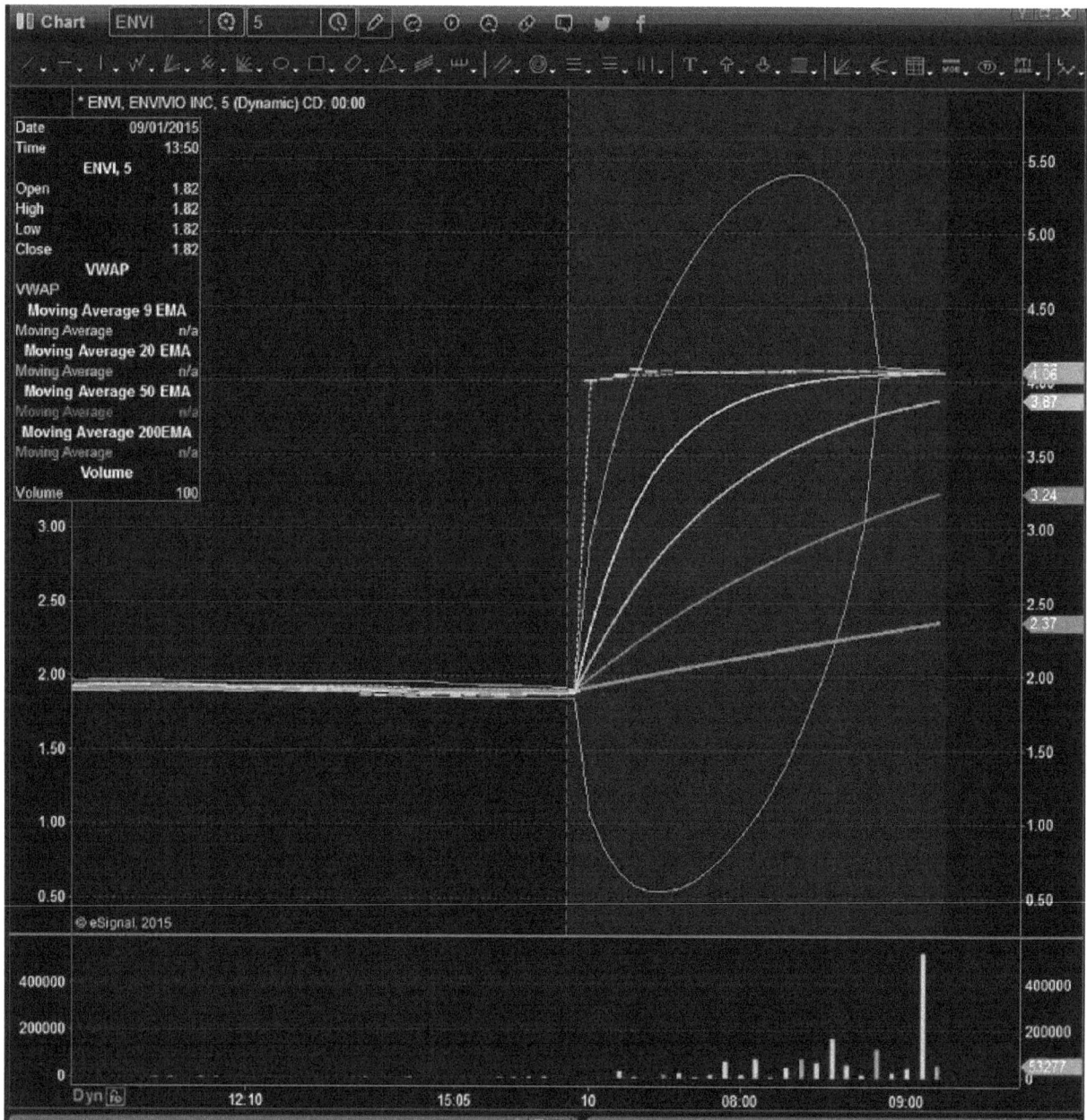

Chart of a stock that has just been bought out.

When we are reviewing the news for a stock, it is important to think about the quality of the source. News released directly from the company, a competing company, majority shareholders, top tier analyst firms or government agencies will typically be the strongest. This will include earnings results, sales contracts, buyout offers, stock buyback programs, FDA approvals, government investigations, patent approvals, etc. News released from unknown analysts or unconfirmed sources should always be considered suspect.

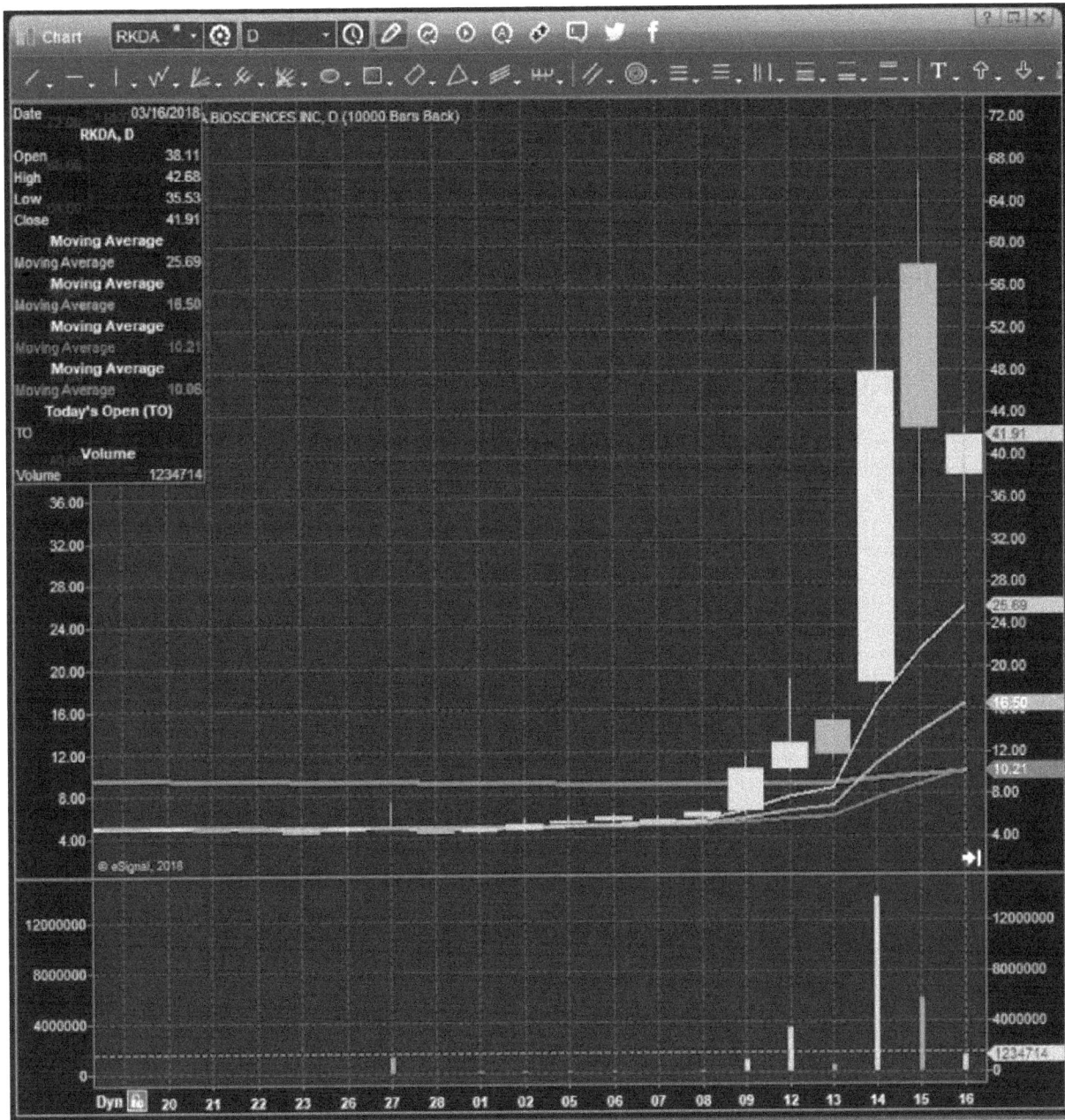

Chart of a Former Runner, a stock known to make huge moves when it has news.

Former Runners

It is important to be familiar with former runners. A former runner is a stock that has made huge intraday moves in the past, or has made parabolic moves on the daily chart. These are stocks that made moves in excess of 100% over a few days. If we notice a former runner reporting news, it is worth keeping a close eye on it. We already know the stock has the potential for home run type breakouts, so it is possible we could see that type of move again under the right conditions. Former runners will typically have all the characteristics of a good stock. They will have that perfect combination of a low float and strong breaking news.

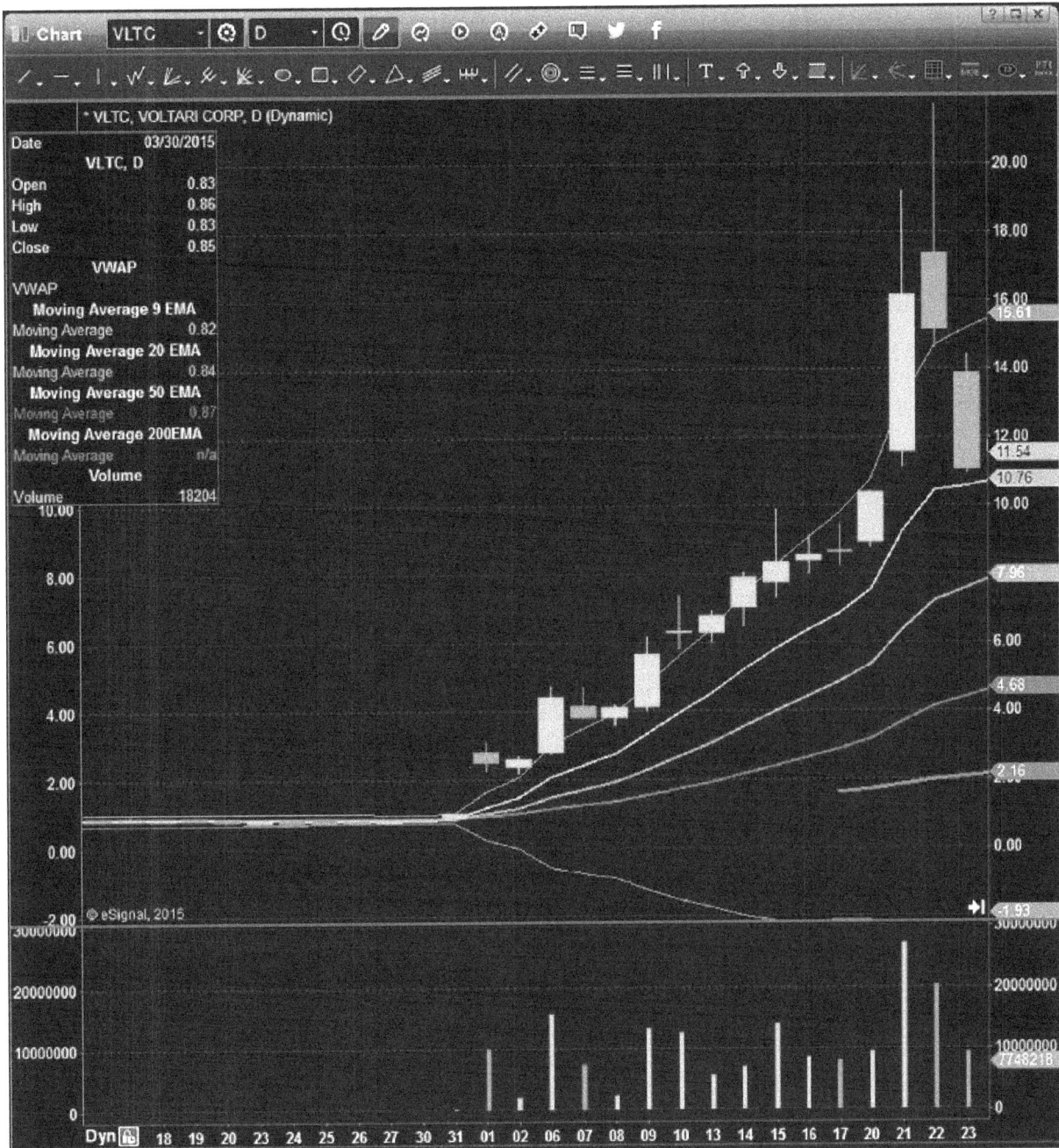

Chart of Low Float Stock moving 10,000% in 3 weeks.

Low Float Stocks

All stocks have a float. The float is the number of outstanding shares available to trade on the open market, not including shares held by insiders and the company. The float is the supply. When a stock makes its initial public offering (IPO), they release a set number of shares into the market. This becomes the float. At any time, a company can begin a stock buyback program to repurchase the shares on the open market. The result of a buyback program will be a decrease in float and typically, an increase in share price. Alternatively, a company can increase their float by selling more shares on the open market through offerings. Selling more shares will increase the float and decrease the value of the shares. Secondary offerings are a form of dilution used for the purpose of raising more capital for the company. This is where the concept of supply and demand in the markets comes from.

Day traders will always want to be aware of the float size of the stocks they trade. If a stock has a great catalyst and a very low float, the supply and demand effect can cause 100% intraday moves. In contrast, a stock that has a very large float is unlikely to result in more than a 10% intraday move, even with the best news. By understanding the float, we can recognize the potential of a stock. Whether we are looking at a pre-market runner or reviewing a stock that just popped up on a scanner mid-day, the float is always going to be one of the first things we check. As day traders, we hunt for volatility, which means we prefer to trade lower float stocks. Investors looking for less volatility and less risk may look for companies with a larger float. This again highlights the unique skill set required for different market participants.

I prefer to trade momentum stocks with a float of under 50 million shares. Stocks with a float of under 10 million shares will produce some of the biggest percentage gainers. There are days when a stock with a 5 million share float will trade more than 20 million shares. That means the entire number of outstanding shares has changed hands four different times. When stocks trade the entire float of available shares, it is commonly known as float rotation. When we see stocks that move 100%-200% intraday, they will almost always experience at least one full float rotation.

When I trade reversals, I will trade any float. A reversal setup that has a great 5min chart with a strong daily chart can be a good candidate regardless of the float. The target on these types of trades will typically be a move back towards the open price. Stocks with a float of more than 500 million shares will typically be less volatile and less interesting for most day traders.

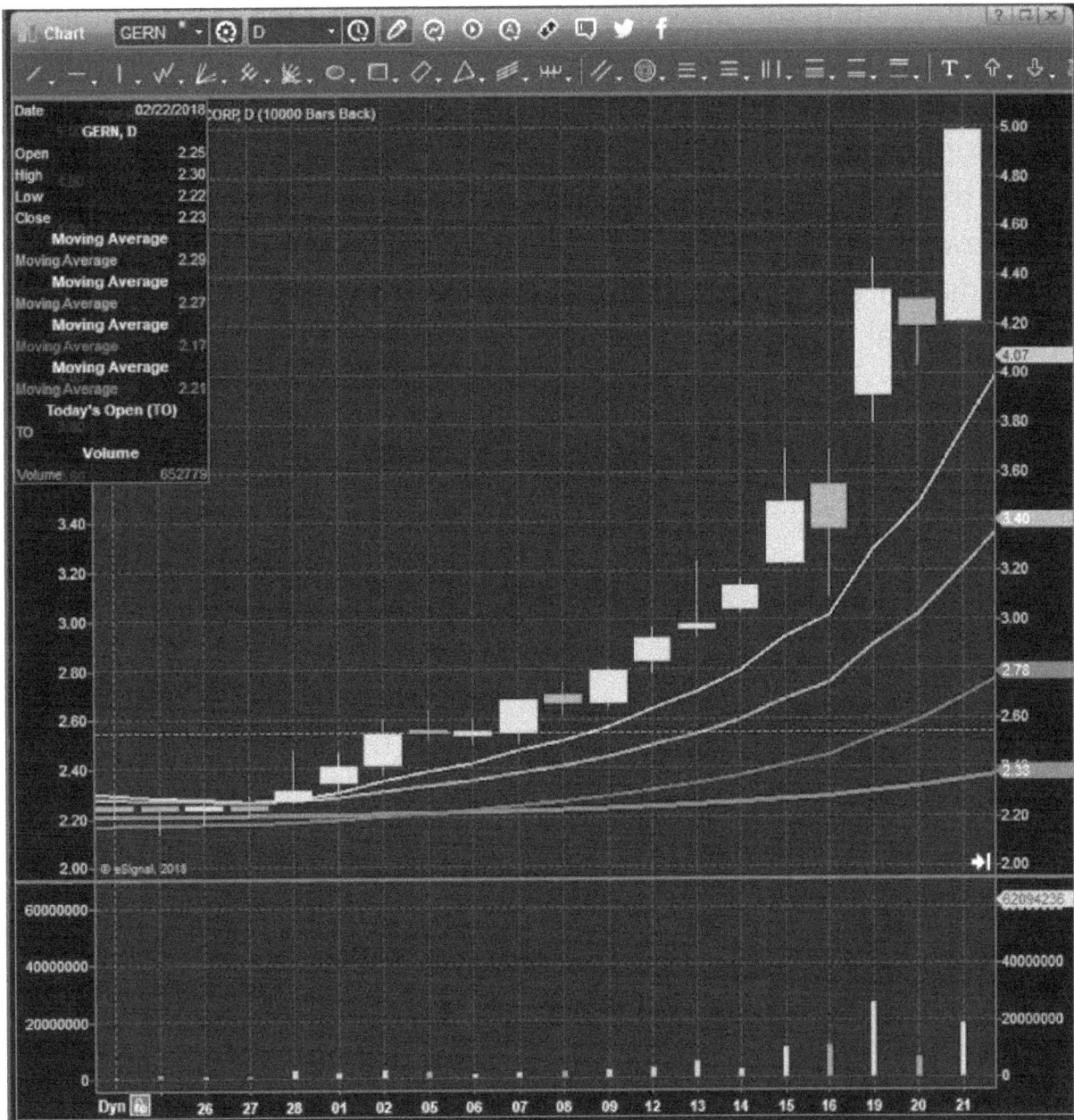

Chart of a several follow through days. This is when momentum continues over several days. A follow through day is when a

candle breaks the previous days high.

Follow Through Days / Continuation

When I review the stocks gapping up each morning, I also take note of stocks that were extremely active in the previous trading day. Sometimes these stocks will have the potential to carry over momentum from the previous day. Multi-day runners are common among stocks that have released really good news and also have strong daily charts. The important price level to watch is the previous days high and low. I only trade when the prices make a fresh breakout versus the previous days high. Typically, the fresh breakout will bring in a new set of buyers and force short sellers to cover their open positions. For this reason, I keep follow through stocks on close watch for a potential breakout.

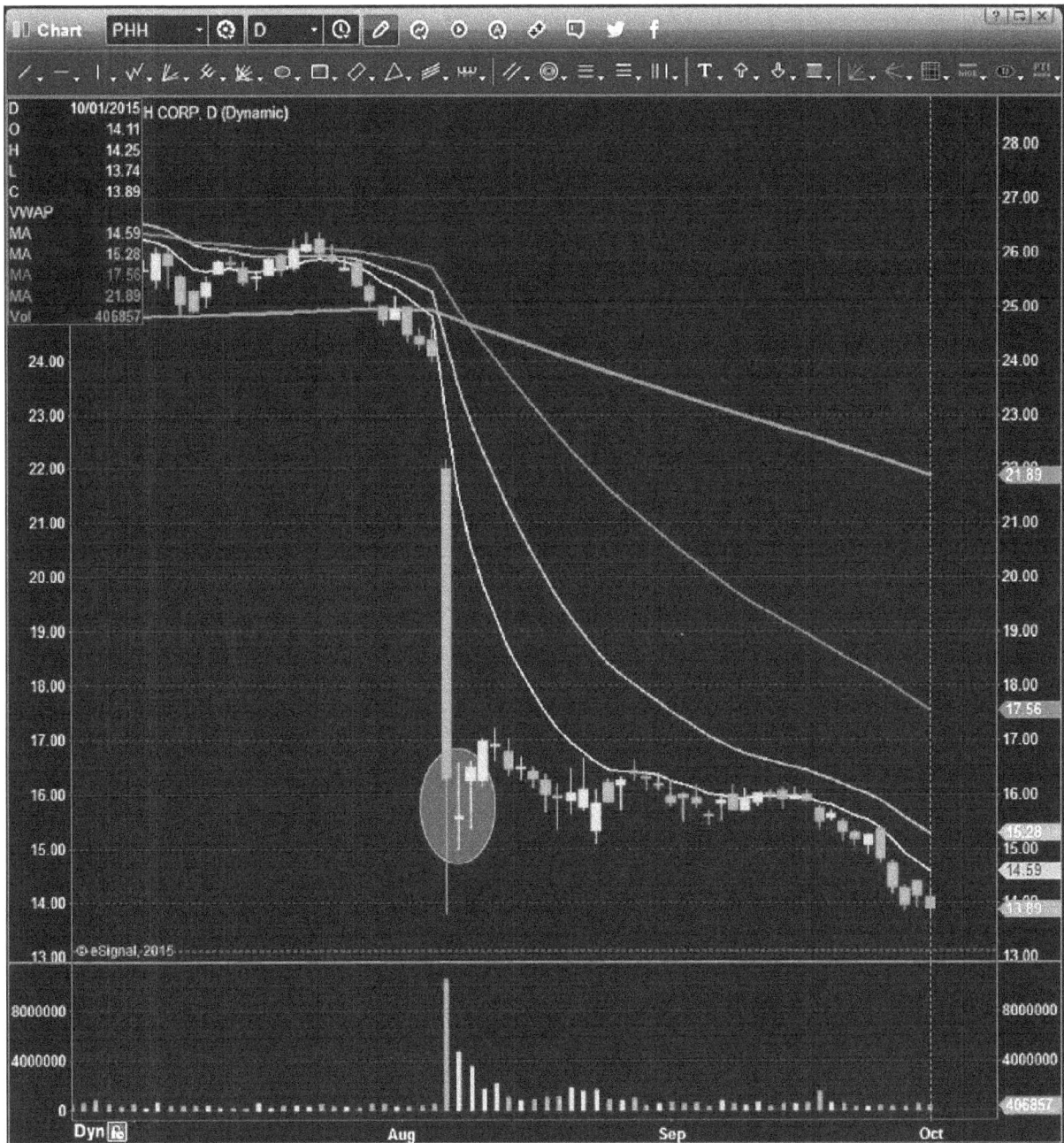

Chart of an inside day. The inside day was the small green candle after the large red candle.

Inside Days

In contrast to follow through days where we look for continued momentum and a fresh breakout, an inside day is when a stock trades completely inside the previous days high and low. I avoid trading a stock on an inside day because there is no reason to expect significant momentum or price action. Inside days will often follow days of big volatility. Sometimes, stocks are able to break out over the previous days range and form a follow through, but until that happens, I stay on the sidelines.

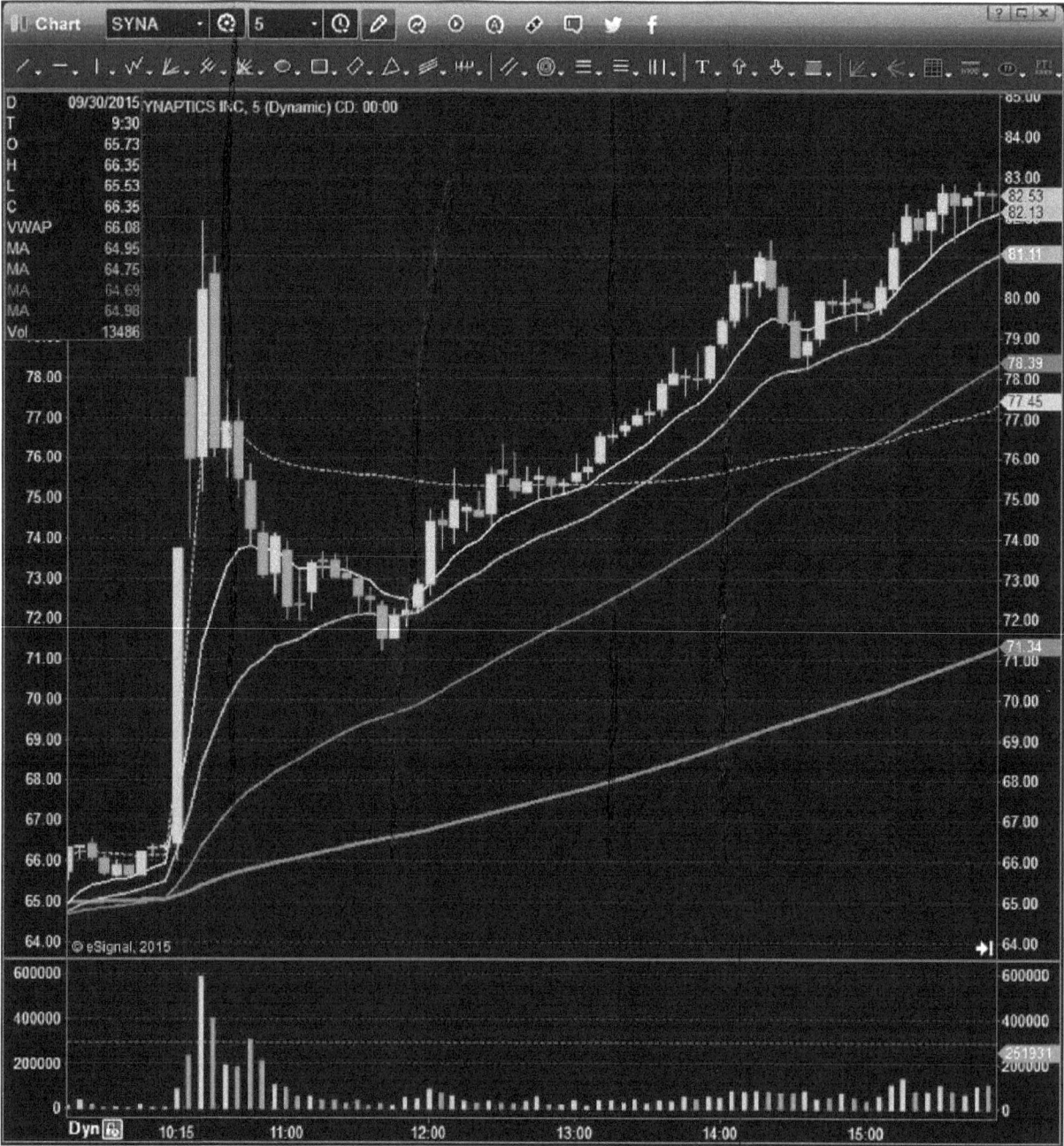

A stock chart showing the power of breaking mid-day news that created a 20 point move. The stock retraces to its moving

averages before finding support and moving back up.

Breaking News & Intraday Extremes

In addition to extreme stocks that are former runners or have low floats, there are also going to be stocks that become irrationally weak or strong in the middle of the day. The midday strength or weakness can sometimes be attributed to breaking news. When news breaks in the middle of the day, it can cause a stock to spike up so rapidly that shares will be halted by a volatility halt. A stock spiking 10% in five minute can trigger these halts. It is not uncommon to see a stock spike up and get halted after a press release. These stocks are experiencing an intraday extreme, and if they are also trading on high relative volume, they become a stock worth watching for a trade. We will apply one of our trading strategies, covered later in this book, to these breaking news setups. In addition to stocks surging on breaking news, we also have stocks that will begin to trade at intraday extremes for no apparent reason. As long as these stocks are trading on high relative volume, they become a stock in play, even if we do not have an obvious catalyst. We would prefer to trade stocks with a clear catalyst, but since we know the market can be irrational, we do not want to discount any stock that is moving with sufficient volume.

Stocks Selection as Risk Management

Trading the right stocks can help reduce your risk as a trader. The majority of stocks in the market are not suitable for day trading on any given day. As day traders, we are only interested in the highly active stocks each day. This means we must be quick to adapt to changing markets. Some months we trade pharmaceutical stocks while other months we trade technology stocks. The market is constantly changing, but we can rest assured that every day there will be a stock trading on heavy volume due to news. Regardless of bearish markets or bullish markets, there will always be volatility in the market and that will keep day traders in business. As hunters of volatility, we begin each day with a review of the pre-market movers and continue through the day with a sharp eye for stocks coming in and out of play. As you continue reading, you will begin to learn about trading chart patterns on the right stocks while applying good risk management principles.

CHAPTER 4

INTRODUCTION TO CANDLESTICKS

As day traders, we spend the majority of our time looking at intraday stock charts, but it's important to remember that every stock is trading in the context of its daily chart. This means that although we will take trades based on intraday chart patterns, we will always keep an eye on potential support and resistance levels on the daily chart. In this chapter, we will work through setting up your basic stock charts and teach the basic chart patterns we look for on daily charts, with an emphasis on support and resistance levels. Later, we will dive into the intraday patterns.

A stock chart is a visual representation of the price history of a stock. Stock charts provide us with a context so we can understand the current price of a stock relative to previous prices. The most commonly used charts for day traders are candlestick charts. If you are looking at a daily chart that includes the last 90 days, you will see 90 candlesticks. On a daily chart, each candlestick represents one day of trading, while on a 1min chart, each candlestick represents one minute of trading. Charts can be set in almost any time frame a trader desires, but the most common time frames are daily charts, 60min charts, 15min charts, 5min charts, and 1min charts. I personally use a daily chart, 5min, and 1min chart to find my entries.

CANDLESTICK BASICS

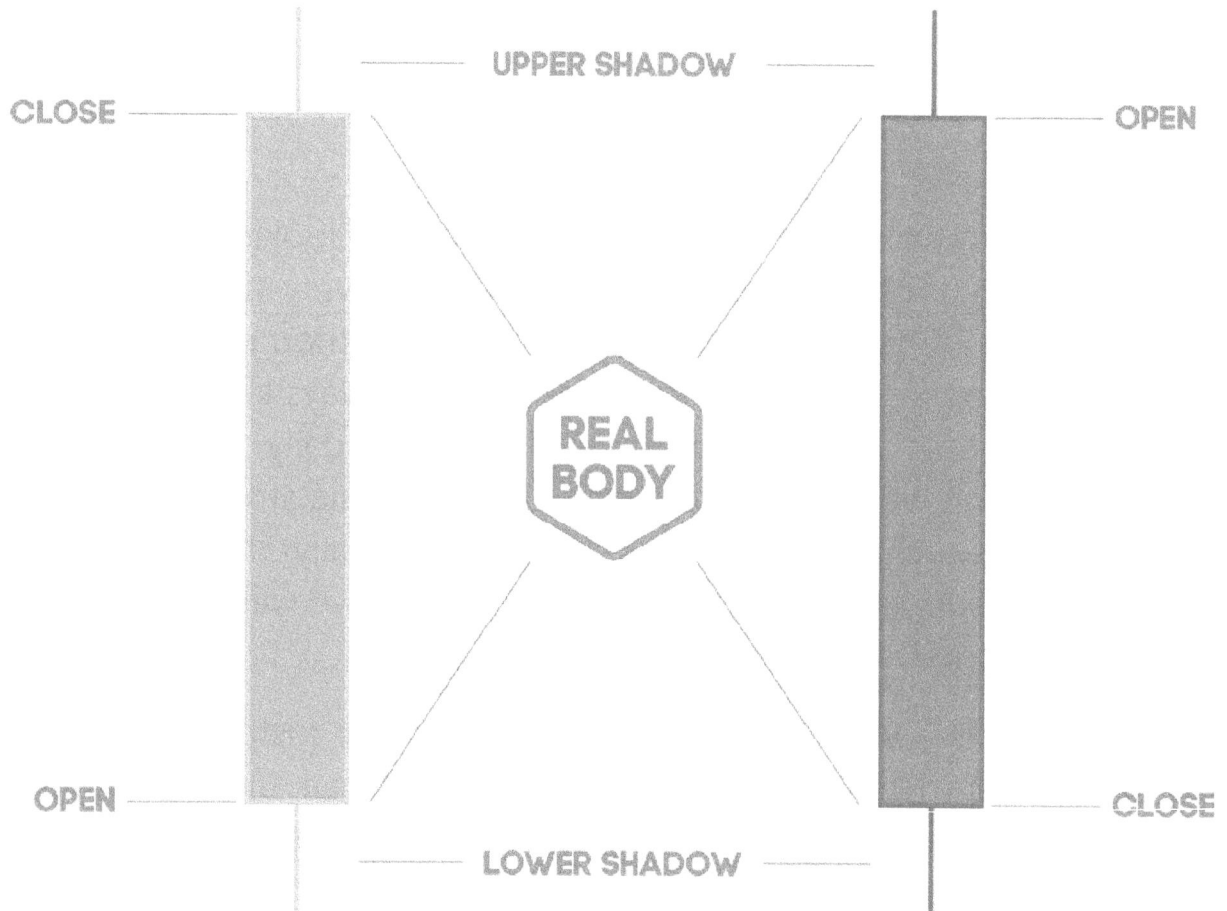

CLOSE ———

UPPER SHADOW ———

——— OPEN

REAL
BODY

OPEN ———

LOWER SHADOW ———

——— CLOSE

A single candlestick provides us with four pieces of information about the price action of a stock within that time frame. The four pieces of information we learn from a candle stick are the high of the period, the low of the period, the open of the period, and the close of the period. The center of the candle is called the real body, and the lines that go up to the high and down to the low are called the upper and lower candle wicks, or shadows. In addition to the four data points, we can also draw conclusions about the market sentiment based on the shape of the candle. Multiple candlesticks lined up together can begin to form familiar chart patterns, including flags and wedges.

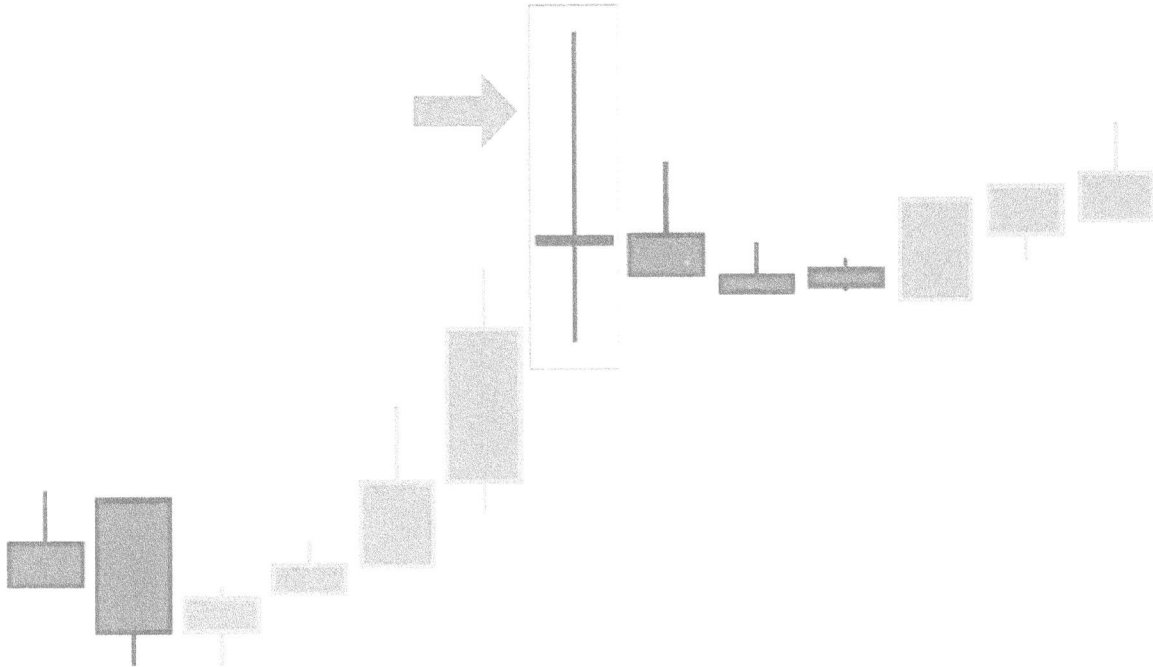

Image of a Doji Candlestick.

Doji Candlesticks

A doji candlestick has a very small candle body, meaning the open price and the close price are nearly the same. We can infer from this candlestick shape that there is a momentary standoff between buyers and sellers. If the candle occurs on heavy volume it tells us there is a battle at that price. Sometimes a doji will also have a long upper or lower candle wick. This tells us the price suddenly moved up or down, but quickly returned to the same price as the open. The means the move was not sustained. In general, doji candles represent some degree of indecision in the market. When a doji candle occurs at the top of a very strong move of 5-10 green candles, the indecision reflected in the candle shape can signify a potential reversal. Doji's that occur during a period of sideways consolidation are less important to us because sideways price action already reflects indecision.

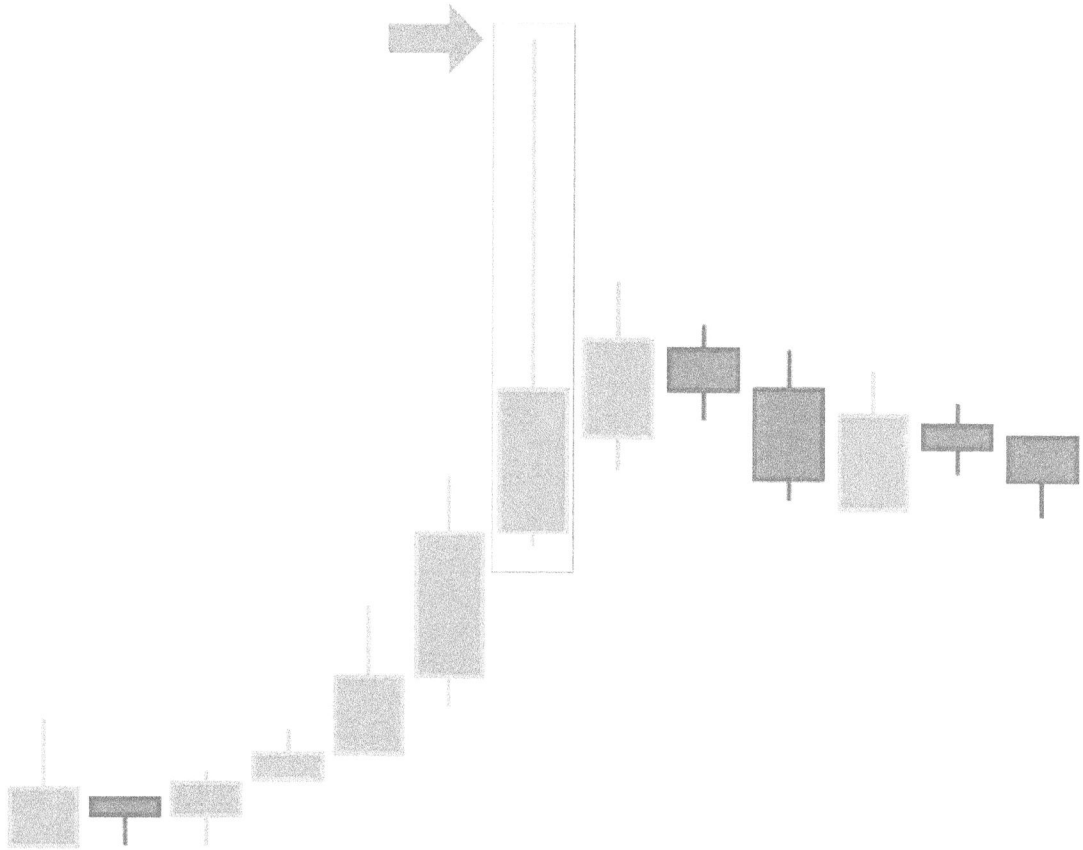

Image of a Topping Tail candle. Bottoming Tails are the inverse candle in a downtrend.

Bottoming Tails and Topping Tails

Candles at the top or bottom of a long trend that have long upper or long lower wicks are considered topping tail or bottoming tail candles. They can signify a potential reversal. The shape of the candle indicates a continuation of the trend, followed by a quick reversal with a close around the middle or low of the candle's range. A doji candle that has long upper or lower wicks is one of my favorite indicators of a potential reversal. I rely on these candlestick patterns for timing my counter trend entries.

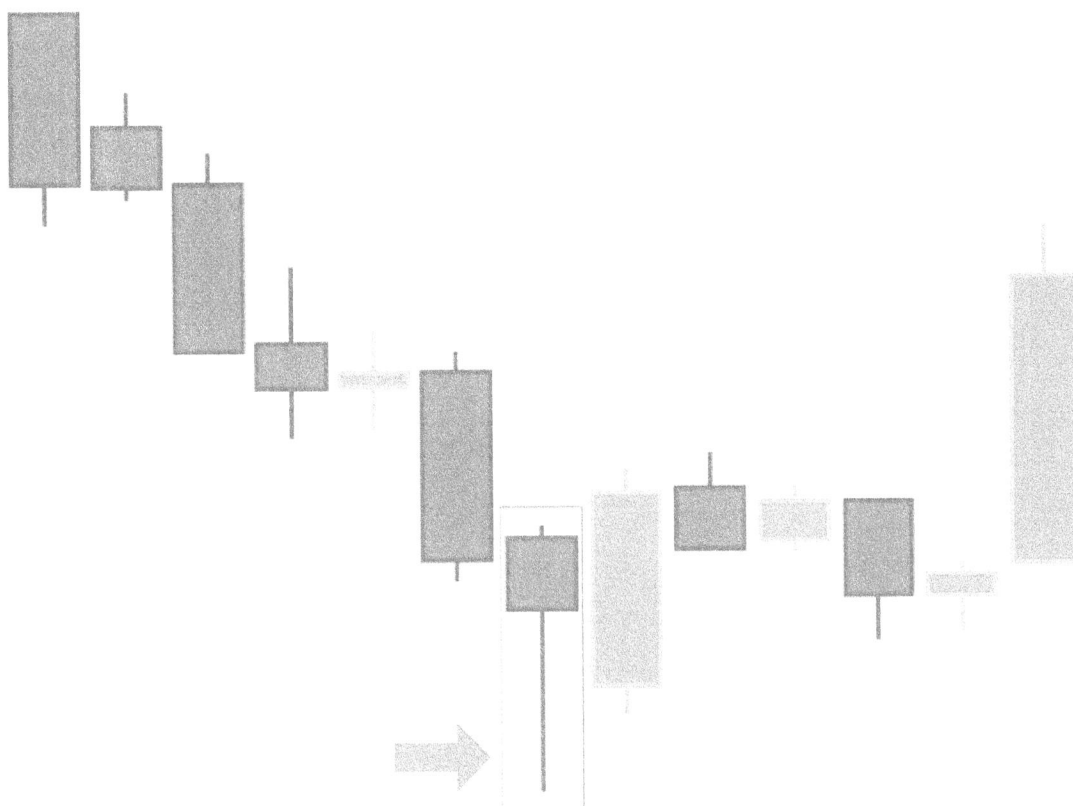

Image of Hammer Candle (inverted hammers occur after uptrend and are upside down).

Hammers and Inverted Hammers

Like bottoming tails and dojis, a hammer candle really only has significance when it occurs in the context of a long downtrend. Hammer candles will always have small bodies and long lower wicks that are larger than the bodies. It is often said that a hammer candle at the bottom of a downtrend is hammering out a new base. The long bottom wick indicates a selloff in that period where the buyers quickly took the opportunity to jump in and push prices back up. This does not always mean the trend will reverse, confirmation of the reversal will come when the next candle breaks the high of the hammer. This is called a candle over candle confirmation. We will discuss the entry and exit indicators in detail a bit later.

An inverted hammer only carries significance when it occurs at the end of a long uptrend. The inverted hammer will have a long topping tail and a small real body. The long topping tail indicates a surge of buying that was quickly reversed. This suggests indecision and a battle between buyers and sellers that was won by the sellers. When we are watching stocks trading in real-time, we can see the formation of the candle wicks. They often appear as a final burst of volume and then a quick and powerful snap back up as the reversal begins.

Long Body Candles

The final candle stick shape we will discuss are long body candles. A long body candle that is green, opens and surges up without ever going down. These candles close at the high and are indicative of extreme bullish sentiment. As day traders, we always want to be holding a stock while a long body candle is forming, but we never want to buy after a long body candle. If we buy at the top of a long body candle we are chasing a large move. Instead, we need to wait for a pullback opportunity if we want to trade with the trend, or wait for a reversal indicator if we want to short the stock.

A red long body candle shows extreme bearish sentiment as the candle opens and sells off for the entire candlestick period. If we are in a short position during the formation of a long body candle, we may want to consider covering part of our position into the flush to the downside. After a series of several long body candles in a row, there is a high likelihood of a bounce. Anytime I miss a move, whether to the upside or the downside, I wait for a good reversal indicator. We will discuss the counter trend trading strategies later in this book, but if you can picture three red long body candles in a row that end with a bottoming tail candle, that is the type of reversal pattern we are going to be hunting for. If that bottoming tail also coincides with a daily support level, we may feel confident taking a candle over candle entry on the first candle to make a new high following the selloff.

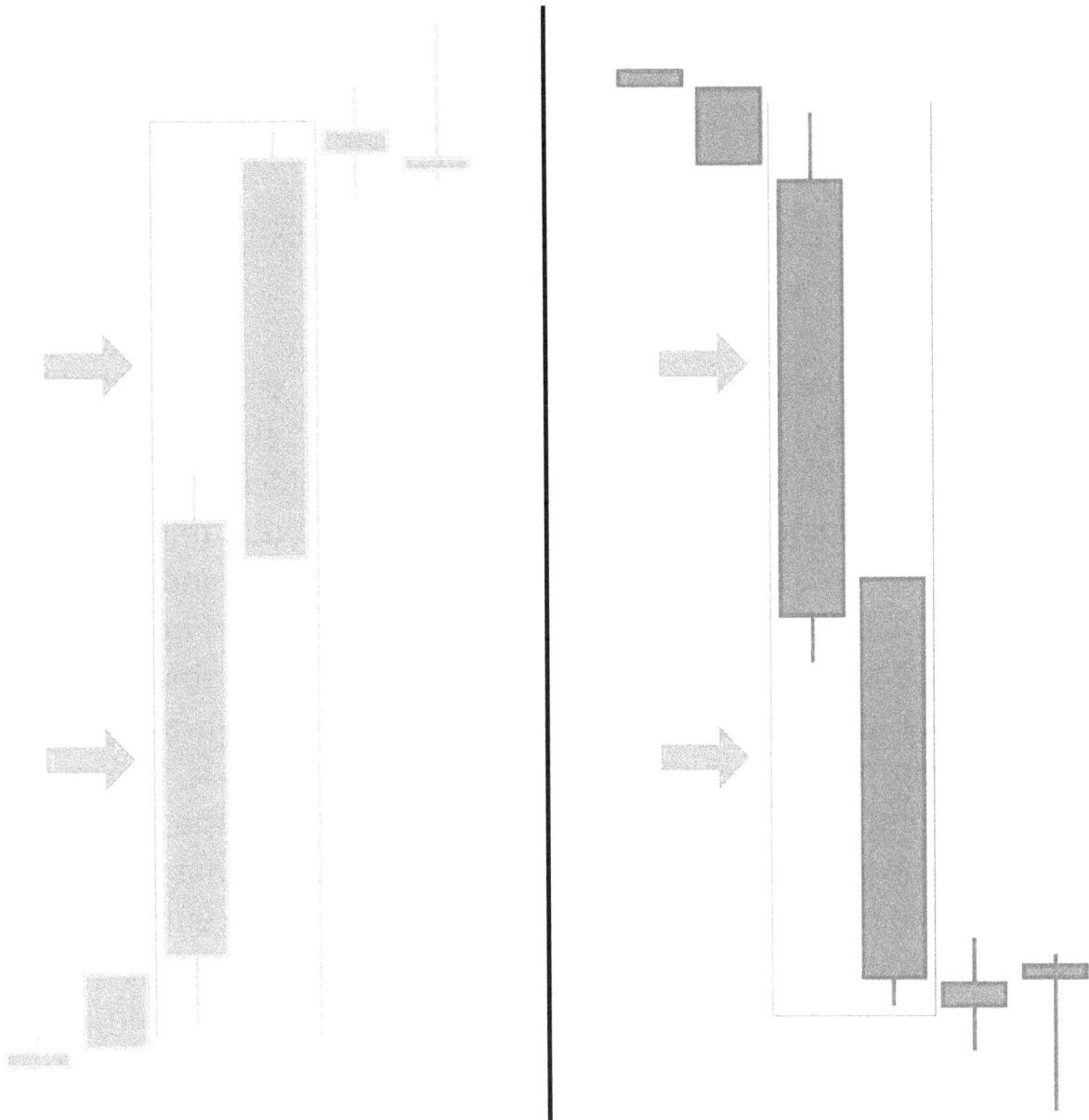

Image of Long Body Candles (these candles can be either red or green).

CHAPTER 5

SETTING UP YOUR CHARTS -
TECHNICAL INDICATORS

As we setup your charts we are going to focus on keeping things simple and clean. Adding complexity to your charts will create unnecessary confusion. There are thousands of technical indicators available to download and install on your chart, but I think they are predominantly overrated and unnecessary. Technical indicators are almost always lagging indicators. They are a middleman between you and the price action. A technical indicator is a formula that calculates current price action and then tries to place the price in a context in order to help predict future price action. The problem is, that by the time a technical indicator is confirming a reversal, the reversal is already well underway. Like with price action, a trader has to learn to anticipate the move before it actually happens. We can either learn to read the subtle cues of an indicator or focus on the candle sticks. I decided I would prefer to become an expert at reading candlestick shapes and patterns than the moves of a technical indicator. We are cutting out the middleman and going straight to the price action. The hunt for the perfect combination of indicators that will give you that added measure of confidence can become dangerously close to the hunt for the Holy Grail. I would encourage you to avoid going down that path and instead, focus on candlestick patterns as your primary source for finding setups. In this chapter, I will introduce you to the technical indicators I use on a daily basis. We will discuss the detailed application of these indicators later in the book.

3 Chart Layout showing 5min, 1min, and Daily charts side by side.

My Chart Layout

When I am looking at a stock, I always have three charts that I am watching. The 1min, 5min, and daily charts. The 1min and 5min charts are zoomed in to show just today's price action, but the daily chart will usually show the last 3-6 months depending on what I am looking for. On the daily chart, I will draw out my horizontal trend lines to mark out windows and triggers. On the 1min and 5min chart, I will draw support and resistance lines throughout the day. I find the visual presence of the lines helps me make decisions about whether a trade is worth taking and how much room for profit it might have.

You will notice that my charts are very clean. I use a few of the most common technical indicators, but I try to keep it really simple.

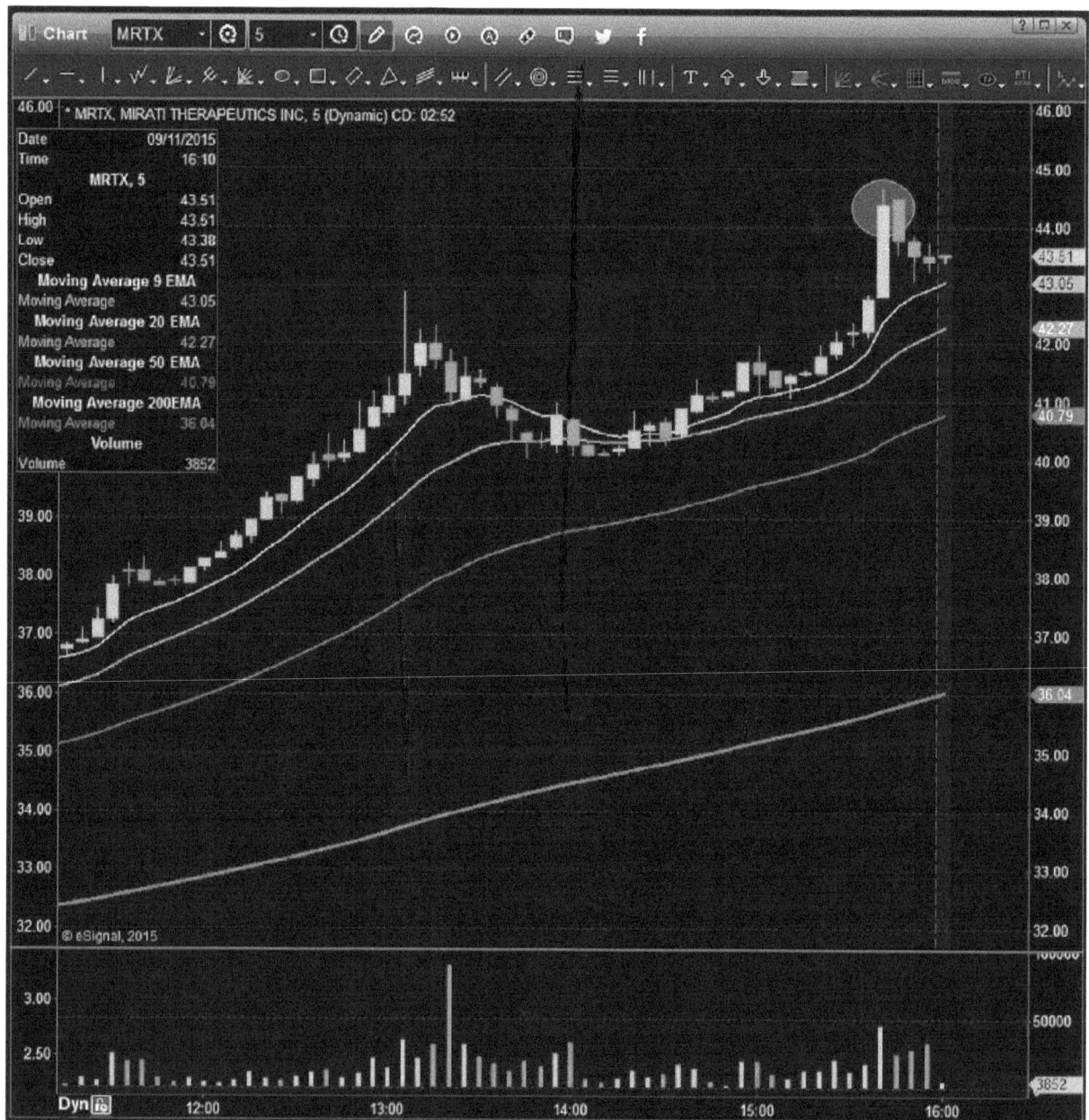

Chart of Moving Averages (Gray is 9 EMA, Blue is 20 EMA, Red is 50 EMA, Purple is 200 EMA).

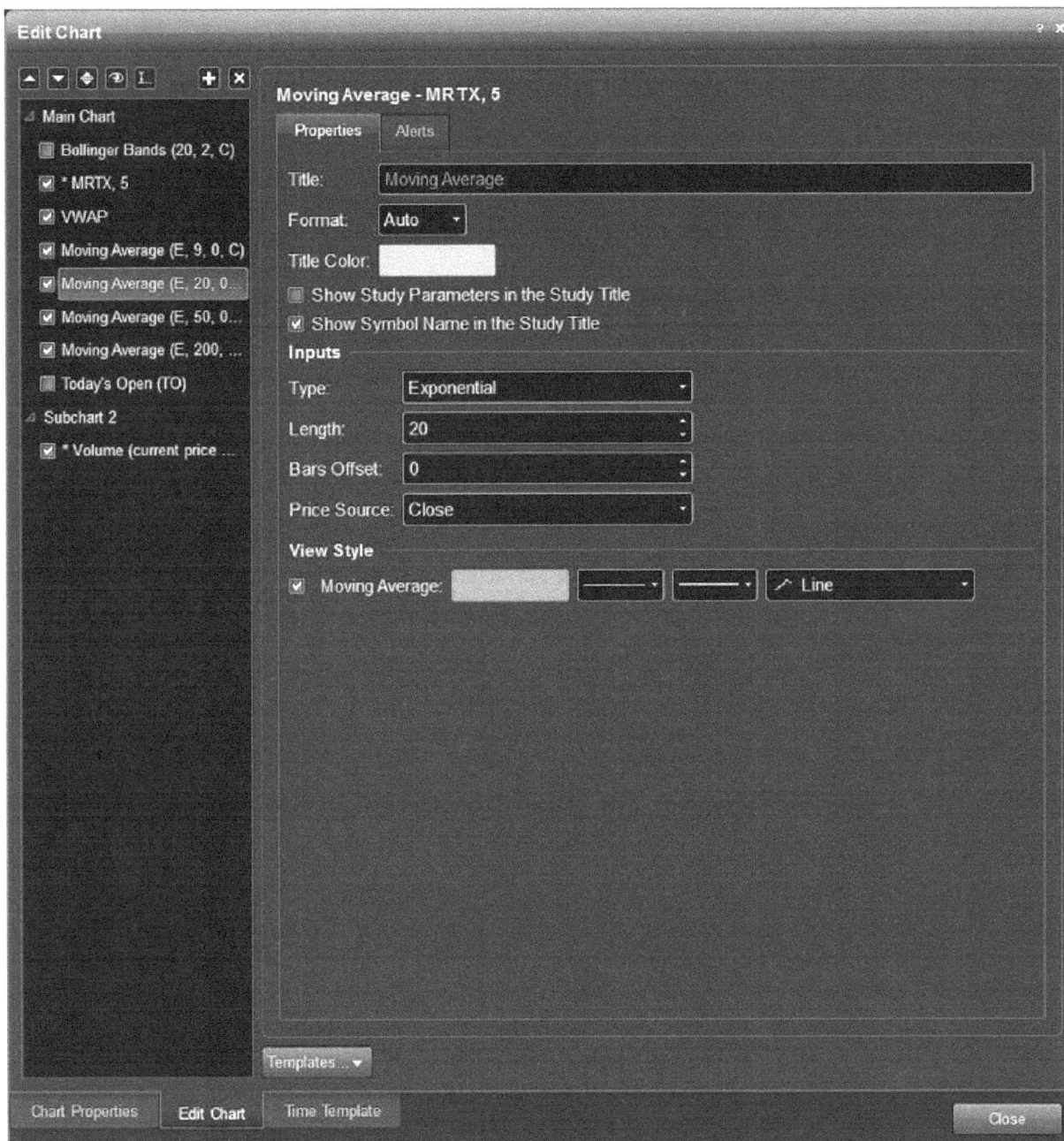

Image of standard Moving Average settings.

Moving Averages

Moving averages are one of the most important indicators I use as a day trader. They represent well respected levels of support and resistance for most stocks on both an intraday and a daily level. While using moving averages alone are not enough to be a profitable trader, they are an important indicator on our charts because they show the direction of the trend. Stocks trading above their moving averages are considered in an uptrend while stocks below their moving averages are in a downtrend. Therefore, when price crosses a moving average there will be a lot of traders that take notice and adjust their positions.

There are two types of moving averages. Simple moving averages (SMA) and exponential moving averages (EMA). All moving averages are calculated as the average price of a stock over a set period of time. A 9 period moving average is based on the last 9 candles. A 9 period moving average on a 5min chart will be different from the 9 period moving average on a 15min, 60min, or daily chart, since the last 9 periods will be different for those time frames. A simple moving average is the average price over the set number of periods. An exponential moving average takes the average over the set number of periods, but will weigh the most recent price action more heavily, so that the moving average moves quickly in response to more recent moves. As a day trader, we are making quick decisions and therefore need an indicator that responds quickly. I use exponential moving averages. The moving averages I have on each of my charts are the 9 EMA, the 20 EMA, the 50 EMA and the 200 EMA.

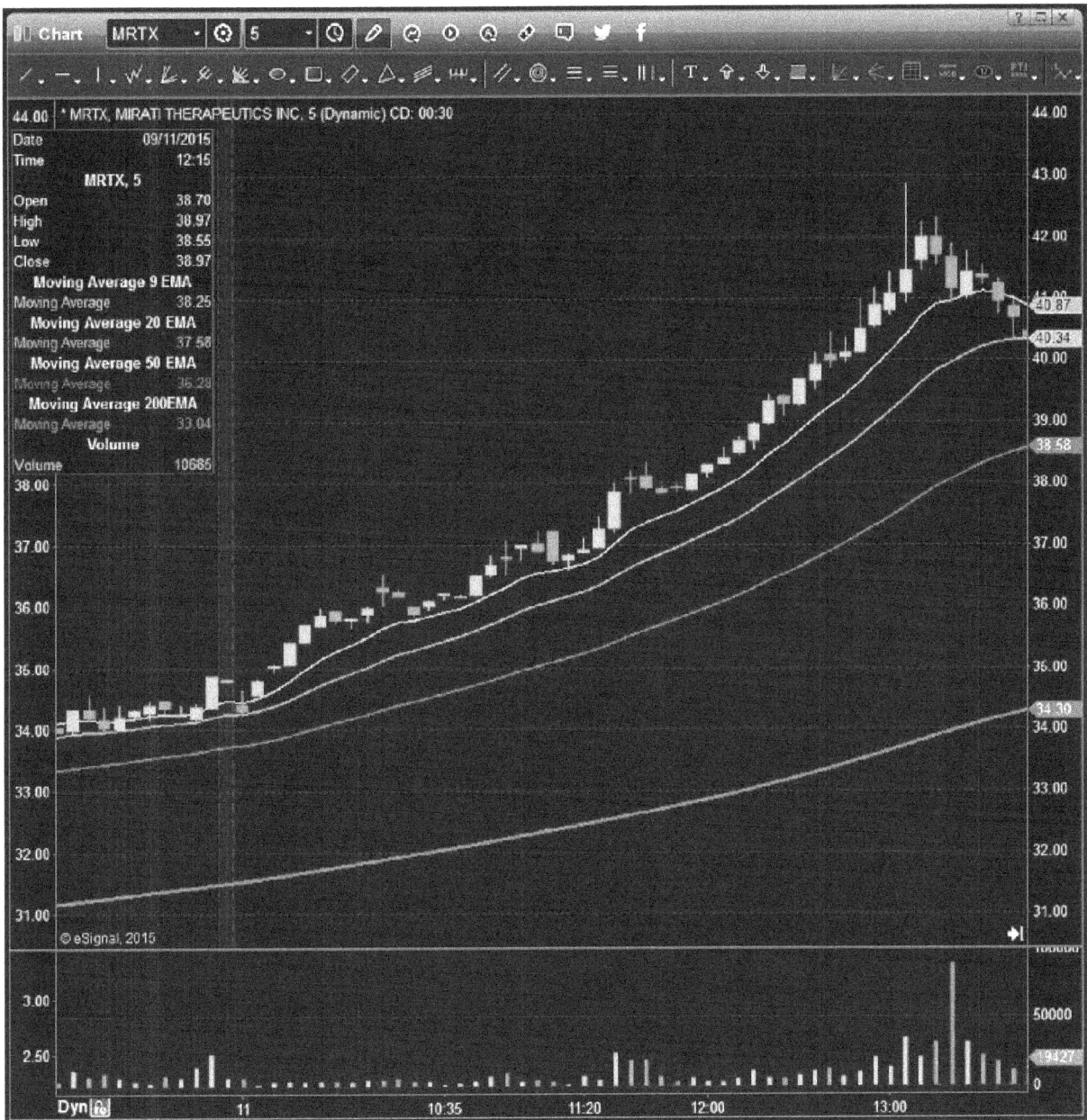

Chart of a stock respecting the 9 EMA (in gray). Each moving average pullback is a buying opportunity. Additionally, the moment the price crosses below the moving average marks a potential change in the trend.

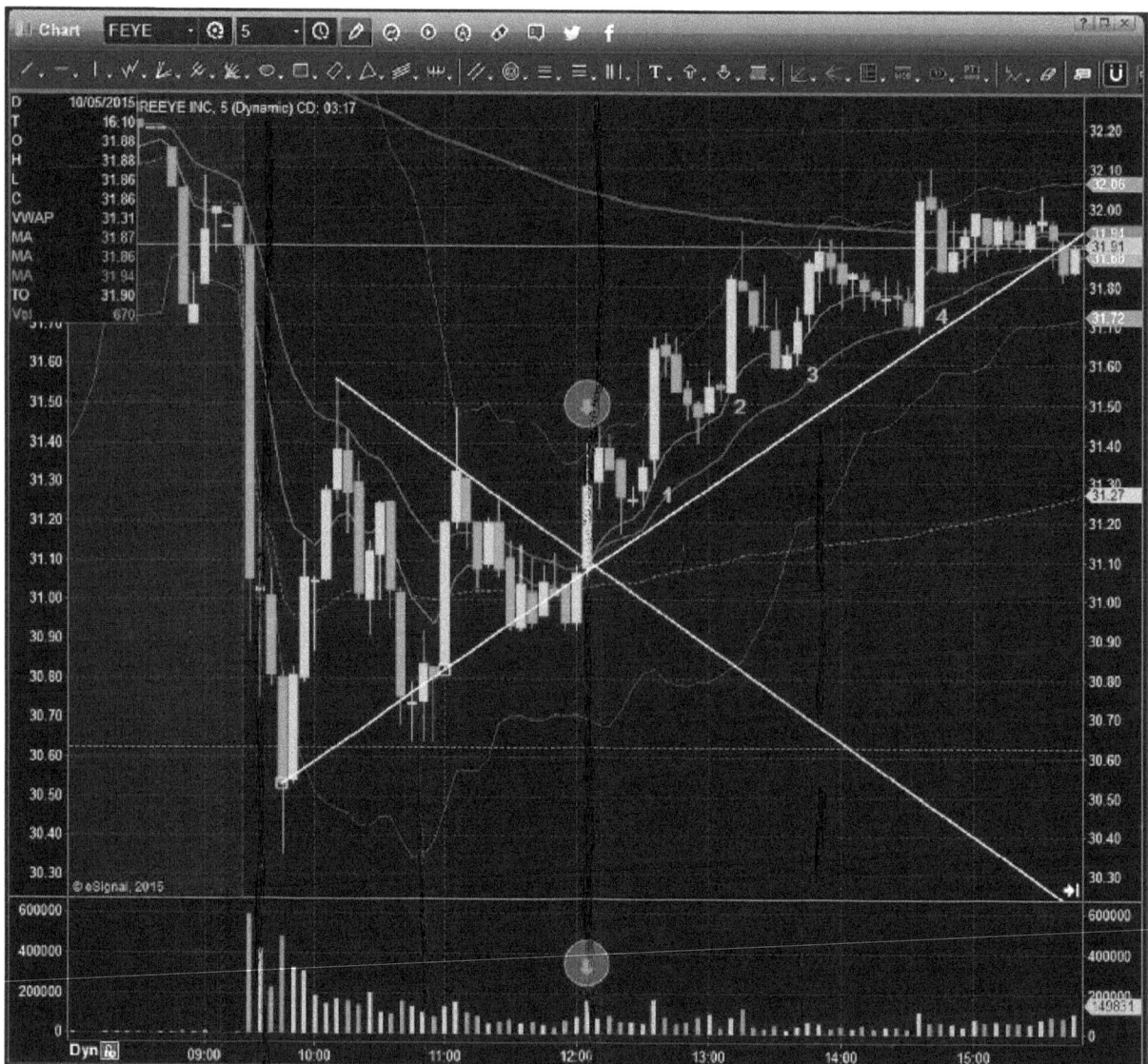

Chart of a trend reversal. The stock was trading below the 9 and 20 EMA, but near the red arrow the price crossed over the moving averages. The first pullback after the price crossed the moving average (labeled #1) took the form of a bull flag and was a great entry. The 2nd, 3rd, and 4th moving average pullbacks were also potential entries.

Trending stocks usually respect either the 9 EMA or the 20 EMA. I prefer to trade stocks trending along the 9 EMA because that shows more strength. Trending stocks will have a pattern of making quick moves up and then consolidate sideways until they tap the 9 EMA, then move back up again. This means if I am in a trending stock, I can set a conservative stop loss slightly below the 9 EMA support level and adjust it as the price moves. Alternatively, if I see a trending stock following this pattern and I want to jump in, I will recognize the moving average as a good potential entry point since it is being respected as support. By entering near the support of the moving average I will typically have a tight stop with good profit potential. When a trending stock makes moving average pullbacks I will typically buy the first and second pullback most aggressively and be a bit cautious on later pullbacks. When stocks are trending, we want to buy as close to moving average support as possible to reduce risk. In contrast, if I am looking to take a reversal trade, I will usually look to take a position when the price is extremely extended and has moved away from the 9 EMA. The plan is to take profits on part of the trade when price comes back to the 9 EMA to test that support or resistance level.

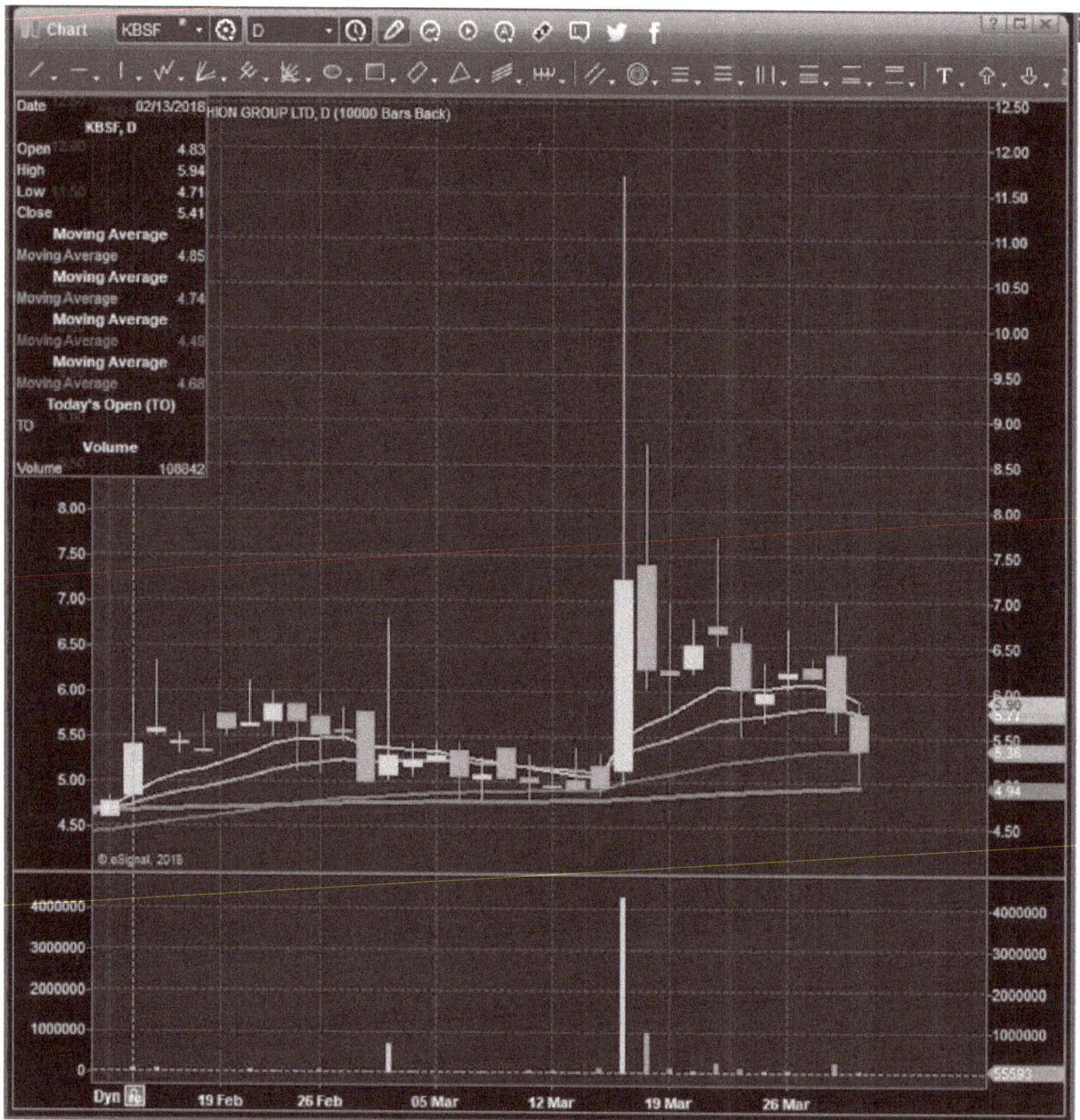

Chart of a stock respecting the 200 EMA (dark purple trend line).

Importance of the 200 moving average

While I primarily use the 9 EMA on my 5min and 1min charts, the 200 EMA is also a very well respected moving average. It is not uncommon to find support or resistance at the 200 EMA on the 5min chart, and especially on the daily chart. I often trade cautiously around the 200 moving average because I recognize stocks may consolidate before breaking away from that level. If I am looking for a reversal trade and the price is running into resistance at the 200 EMA I would consider that to be a stronger setup. Most of the momentum trades I take will be well above the 200 EMA. I rarely take trades to the long side that are below the 200 EMA or take trades to the short side that are above the 200 EMA.

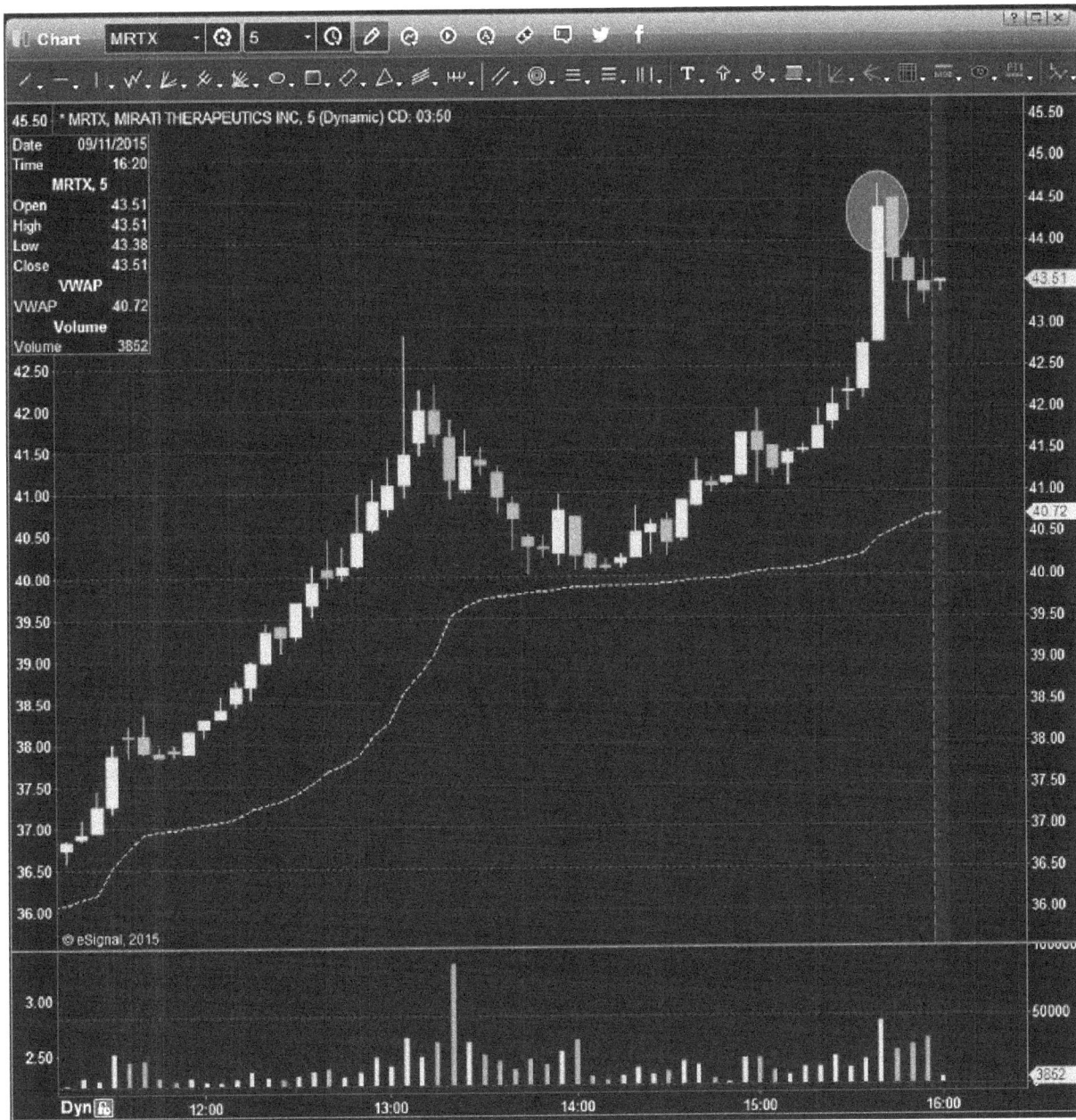

Chart of the VWAP indicator.

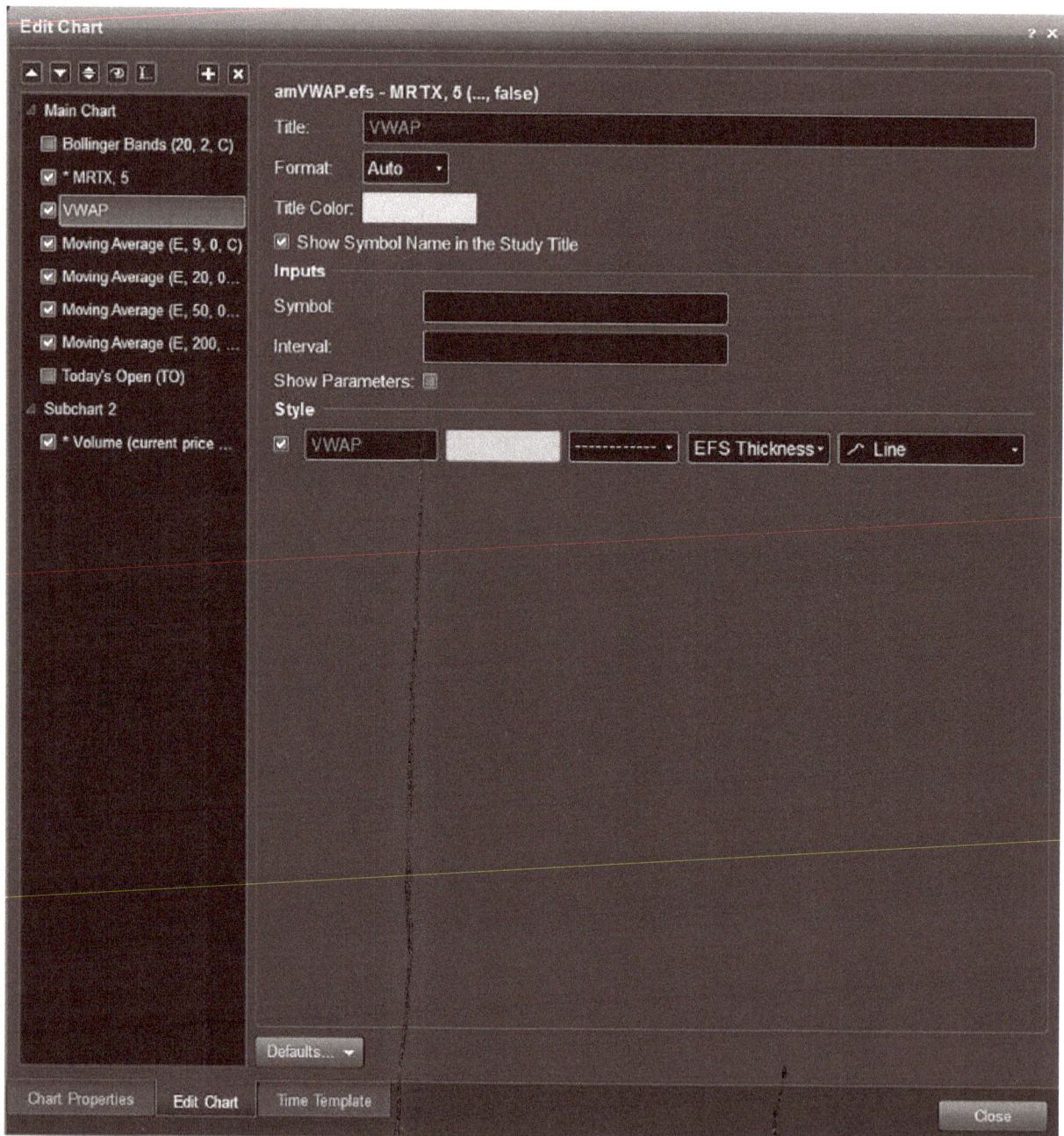

Image of standard VWAP settings.

Volume Weighted Average price (VWAP)

In addition to the standard moving averages, I use the Volume Weighted Average Price (VWAP). Just as the exponential moving averages give weight to recent price action, the VWAP weighs the amount of volume that traded at each price more heavily. The VWAP gives us a really good understanding of the average price of the stock over the course of the day, because it factors in how many shares were traded. The VWAP is the equilibrium point of a stock on any given day. If we are looking for countertrend setups, we would want to find a stock that is extremely extended away from its equilibrium point. For trend based trading, I generally look to find entries close to the VWAP. This is not always possible if a stock has made a really strong intraday move. In cases where the price is extended from the VWAP, but I still want to take a trend based trade, I will refer back to the price relative to the 9 EMA.

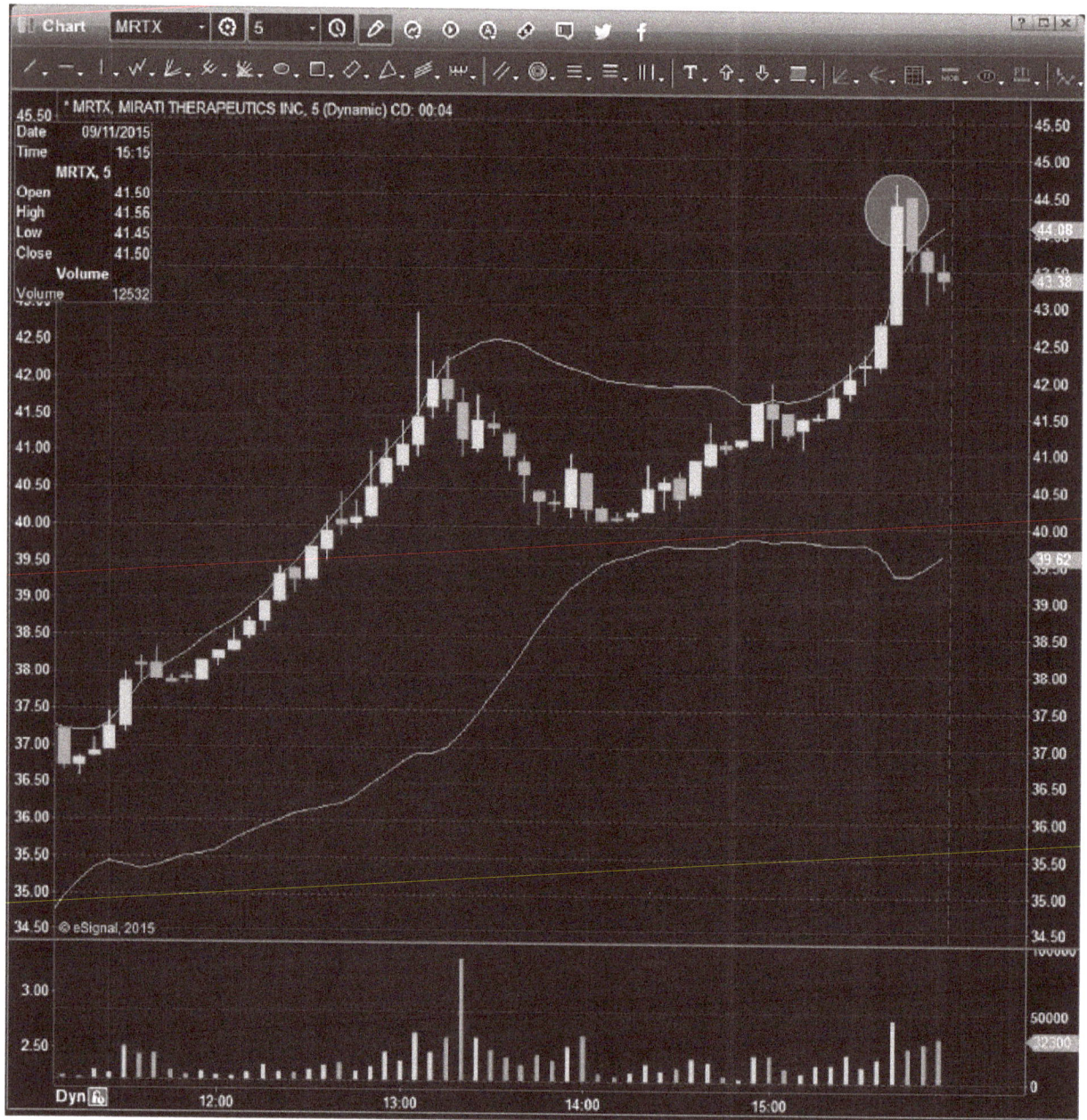

Chart with Candle outside Bollinger Bands.

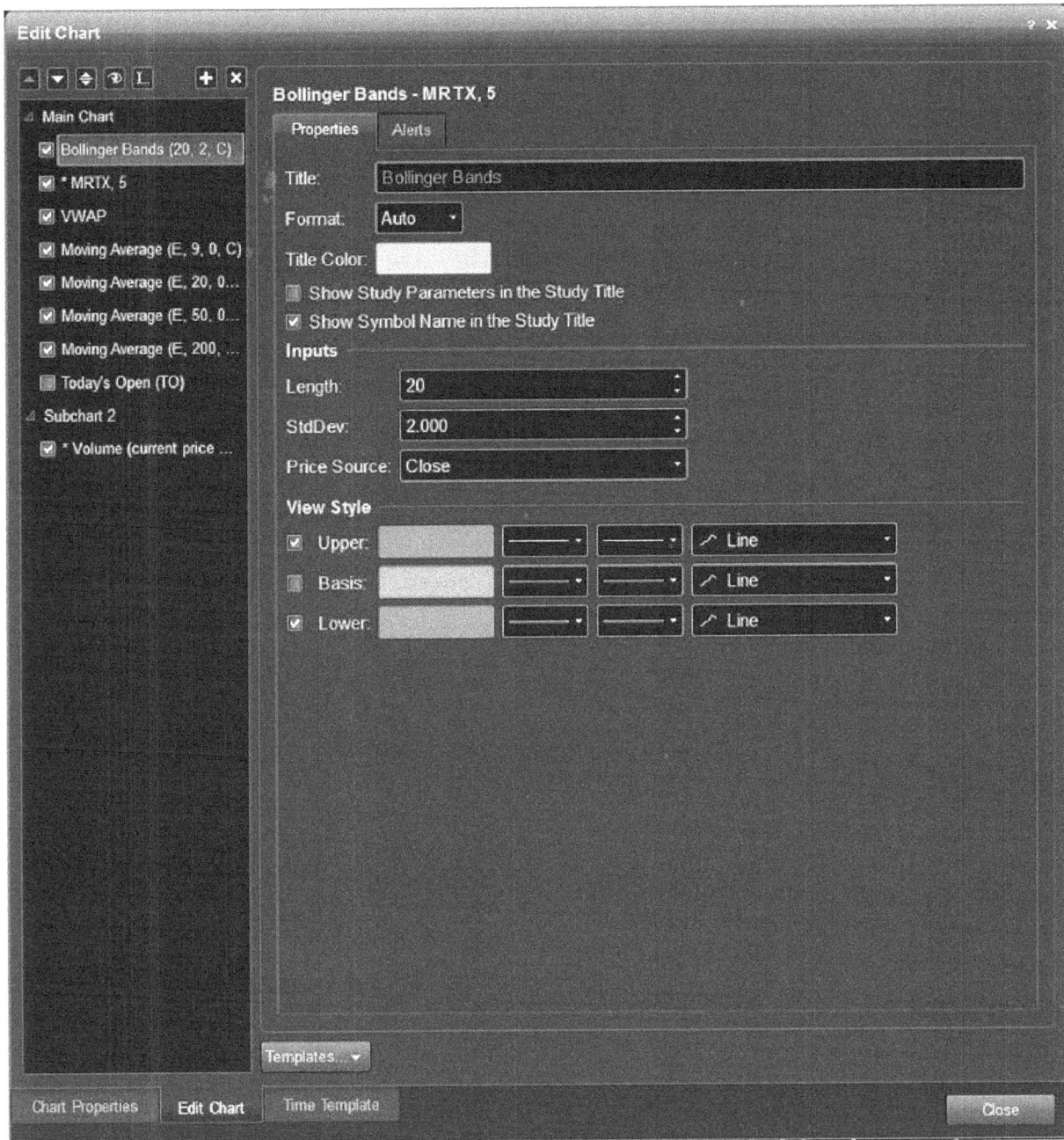

Image of standard Bollinger Bands settings.

Bollinger Bands

I use Bollinger Bands exclusively for timing reversal trades. I use a standard 20 period moving average with a 2.0 standard deviation for my Bollinger Bands. This is the default setting for the indicator. As a counter trend trader, we have to be very careful not to enter a reversal trade too soon. We want to enter stocks as close to the maximum extension point, and then ride the momentum when the trend reverses. In order to get good entries, I wait for candles to trade outside the Bollinger Bands. You will notice that almost all of the price action on any given day will take place inside the Bollinger Bands. Therefore, anytime the price is outside the Bollinger Bands, it's an extreme situation. It is important to remember that prices can stay outside the Bollinger Bands during a parabolic move, so we still have to be cautious about entering too soon. The reason we trade intraday extremes, like candles outside Bollinger Bands, is because we know this is where we will find above average volume. In order to make sure any reversal is trading at extremes, I keep the Bollinger Bands on my 5min charts. I do not use them on the daily charts or the 1min charts.

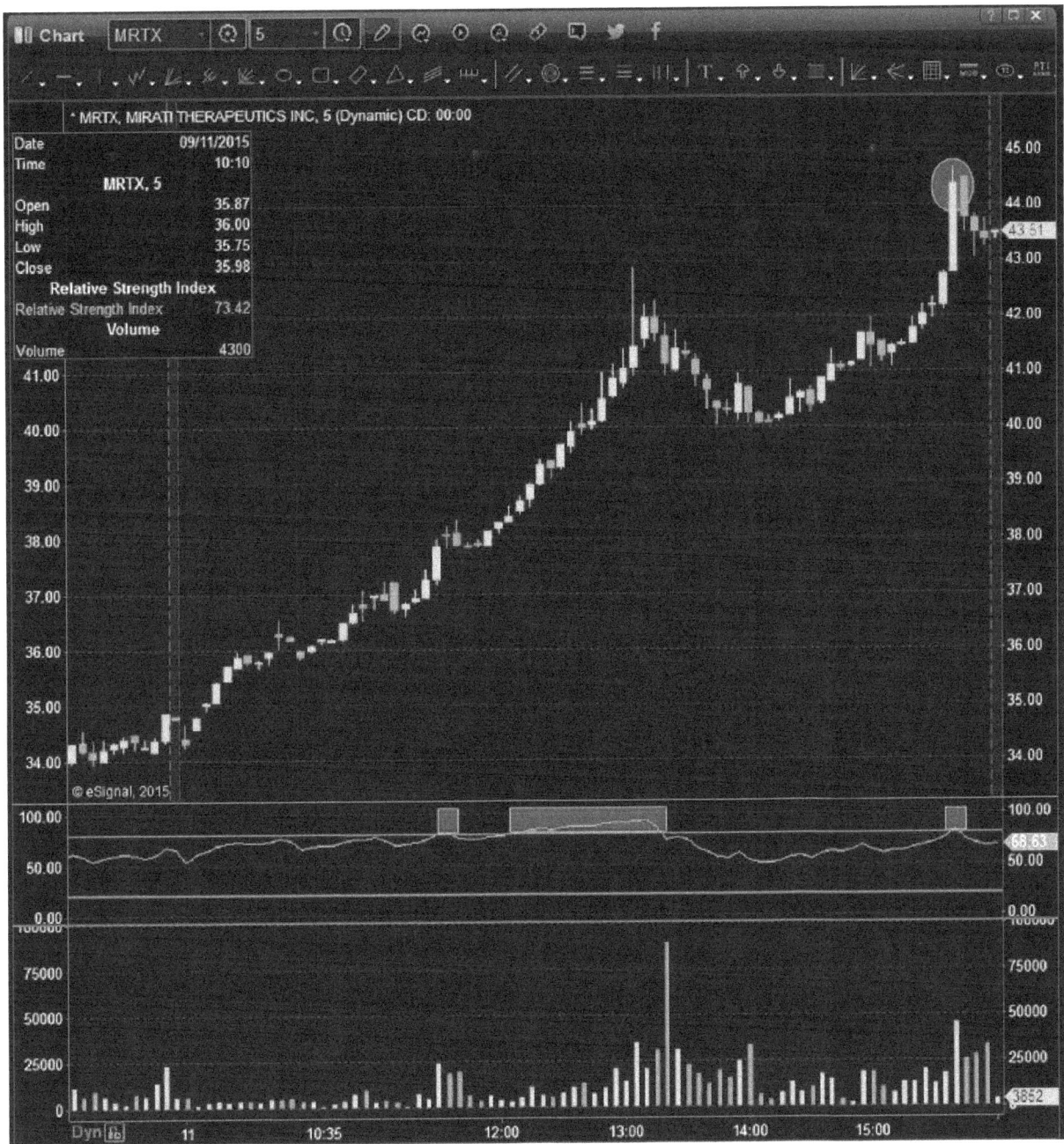

Chart with Relative Strength Index.

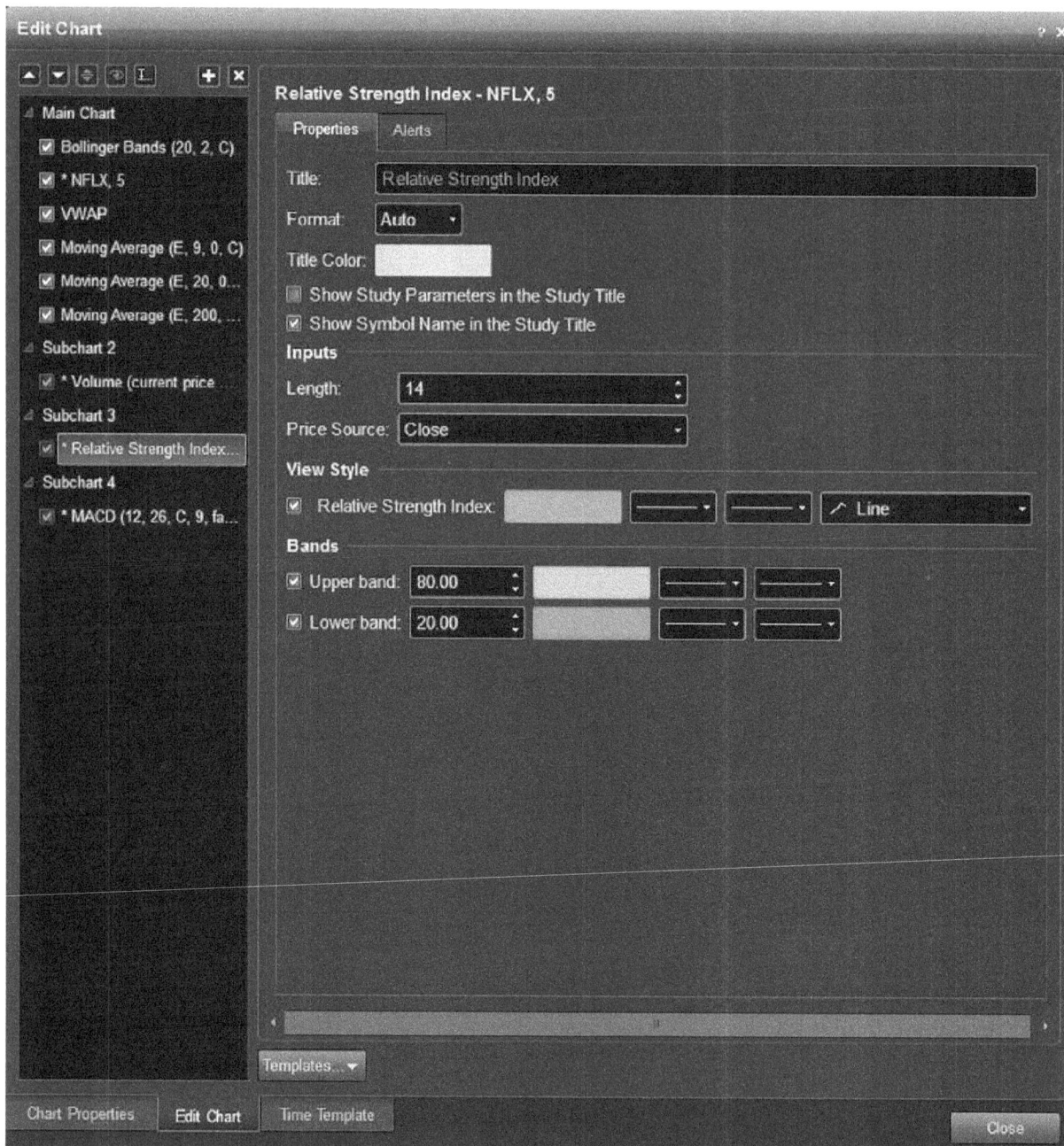

Image of standard RSI settings.

Relative Strength Index (RSI)

I use the Relative Strength Index (RSI) exclusively for reversal trades. Like a candle fully outside the Bollinger Bands, when RSI is below 20 or above 80, it indicates an intraday extreme. Many of best reversal trades will have an RSI below 5 or above 95. RSI is measured on a scale of 0-100, and it represents the strength of the stock. A reading of 90 or 95, indicates an extremely overbought condition while 5-10, represents an oversold condition. Many traders jump to the conclusion that when RSI is at extremes, the trend cannot possibly get any more extended and could change directions. It is important to note that since RSI can remain at extremes for a long period of time, it is not a reliable buy or sell indicator without additional confirmation. Stocks that are trending slowly, up or down, generally don't always show RSI extremes. The RSI extremes are more often combined with parabolic moves or long trends that finally peak with one last surge. Instead of keeping RSI on my charts, I have created a filter in my stock scanners to only show me reversal stock ideas when the RSI is below 20 or above 80.

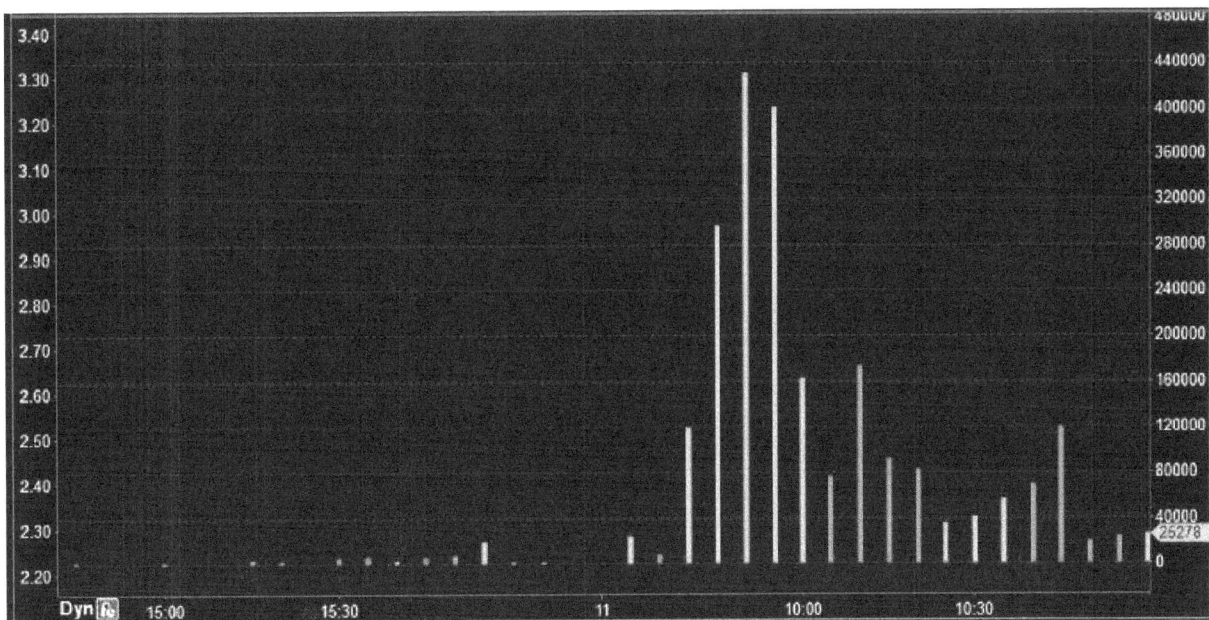

Image of Volume Bars.

Volume Bars

The final technical indicator that I use on a daily basis are simple volume bars. These bars tell us how many shares of volume were traded during a candlestick period. Volume is a critical piece of information for my trading strategies. It would be very difficult for me to trade without the volume bars. I need to have a sense of the increasing and decreasing volume as momentum builds and then fades. When I see decreasing volume during a trend, it can be an indicator that the trend is about to change directions. Additionally, during periods of consolidation, seeing an increase in volume can suggest a potential break back into a trend.

CHAPTER 6

Now that you have a basic understanding of candlestick charts, we will discuss the importance of looking for daily chart patterns. We know that each candlestick represents one day of price action on the daily charts. Whenever I am trading, I typically look at about 3-6 months of trading history on the daily charts. I always keep a daily chart up for each stock I am trading. Remember, that as a day trader, our primary focus will be on finding chart patterns on 1min and 5min charts. However, all intraday charts exist in the context of their daily chart. This means we have to keep an eye on nearby daily support and resistance levels that could come into play. All charts will have price levels of support and resistance, and it is important that you know how to identify these levels. Since the critical support and resistance prices will be respected by professional traders, if you do not realize where they are, you may end up buying when and where everyone else is selling. Plotting price history on stock charts is a form of technical analysis. In contrast to fundamental analysis where we place trades based on the strength of a company, technical traders base trades on chart patterns and indicator readings. As momentum day traders, we are looking for technical breakout patterns. Remember that volume will always be the confirmation that the breakout is real. Without volume, the breakout typically will not be sustained.

I am a strong believer that a great daily chart will provide day traders with setups that have home run potential. However, I have seen thousands of stocks make incredible intraday moves, despite a poor daily chart with a lot of resistance. This will happen when there is such a strong catalyst that it overrides all daily resistance levels. For example, imagine a pharmaceutical stock that has a lot of daily resistance, but has just developed the cure for a previously incurable disease. The news is so great, that the daily chart becomes almost irrelevant as traders scramble to get a piece of the action. This is a good time to remind you that stocks can be irrationally strong or weak! Sometimes, stocks are strong beyond what the fundamental analysis of the company could possibly project. This shows a disconnect between the fundamentals and the actual behavior of a stock. We have to think like a trader and focus on trading the chart patterns. If a stock is continuing to show bullish sentiment and has no indication of reversing, there is no reason to sell a long position or begin a reversal trade. While we will review the important levels you need to understand on daily charts, it is also important to remember that a strong catalyst will typically override a weak daily chart. Conversely, a weak intraday catalyst will rarely breakout despite a strong daily chart because a weak catalyst results in low volume and lack of retail interest. The best breakouts occur with high relative volume, if there is no volume, there will be no trade.

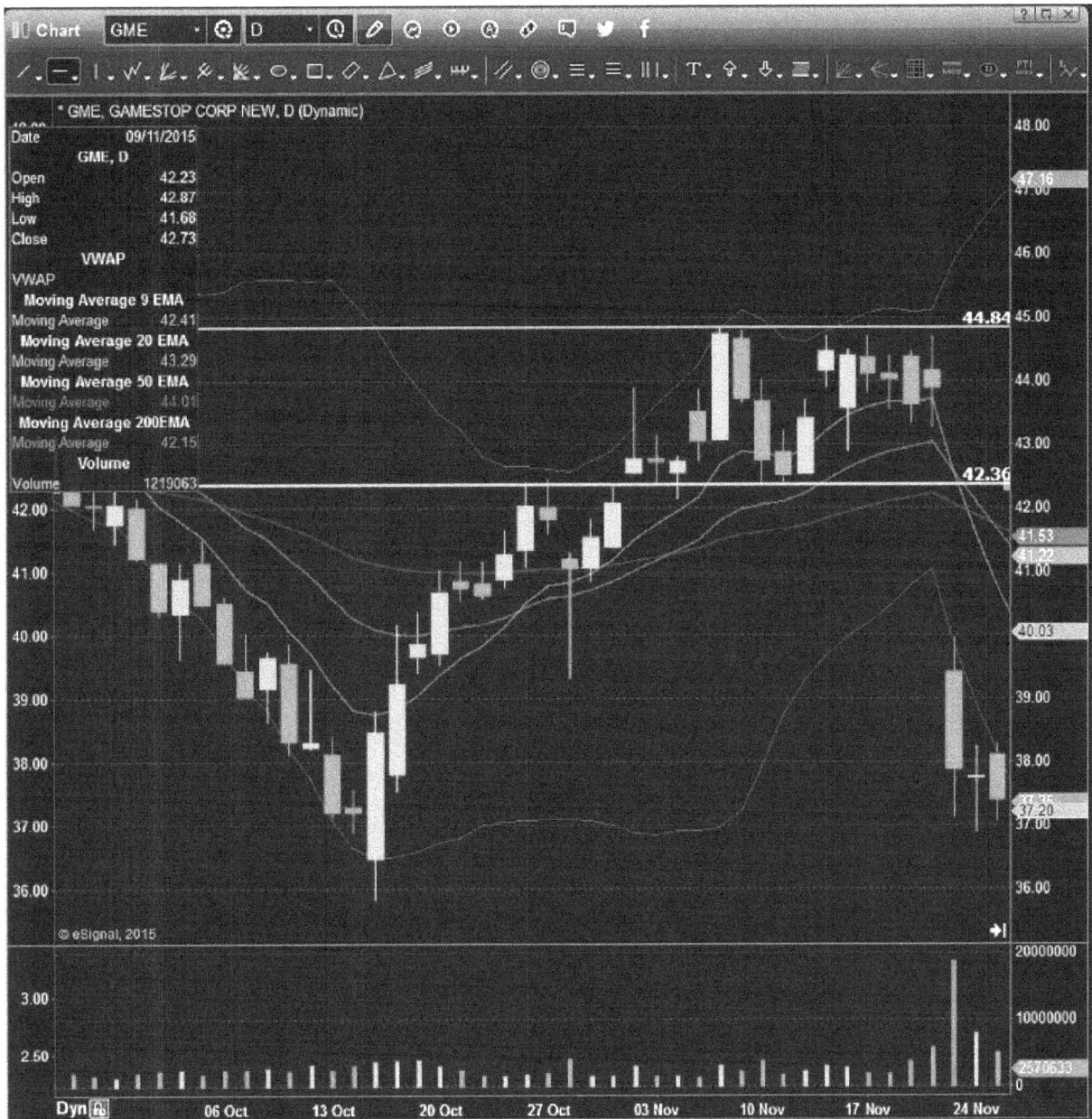

Daily Chart - Recent Support and Resistance Levels.

Support and Resistance

Support and resistance levels are formed when a stock repeatedly touches a price and is unable to break that price. When this occurs to the downside we call that a support level. When it occurs to the upside, we call that a resistance level. Support and resistance levels gain validity the more times a stock touches the level without breaking it. If you pull up a daily chart for any stock you should be able to draw horizontal lines where you can see critical levels that are being respected by traders. Occasionally a level will break briefly and then prices will quickly reverse. This is called a false breakout. Day traders have to be very cautious of false breakouts because we are often taking positions before the breakout has been confirmed. If we wait to take our position until we have confirmation, the breakout has already happened and we will have missed a lot of the profit potential. For that reason, learning to anticipate potential breakouts and learning to recognize signs of a false breakout will be an important skill for any trader. Additionally, by understanding support and resistance levels, we can develop a long or short bias on each of the stocks on our morning watch list. This will help determine the potential of the trades and the type of setups you will be looking for.

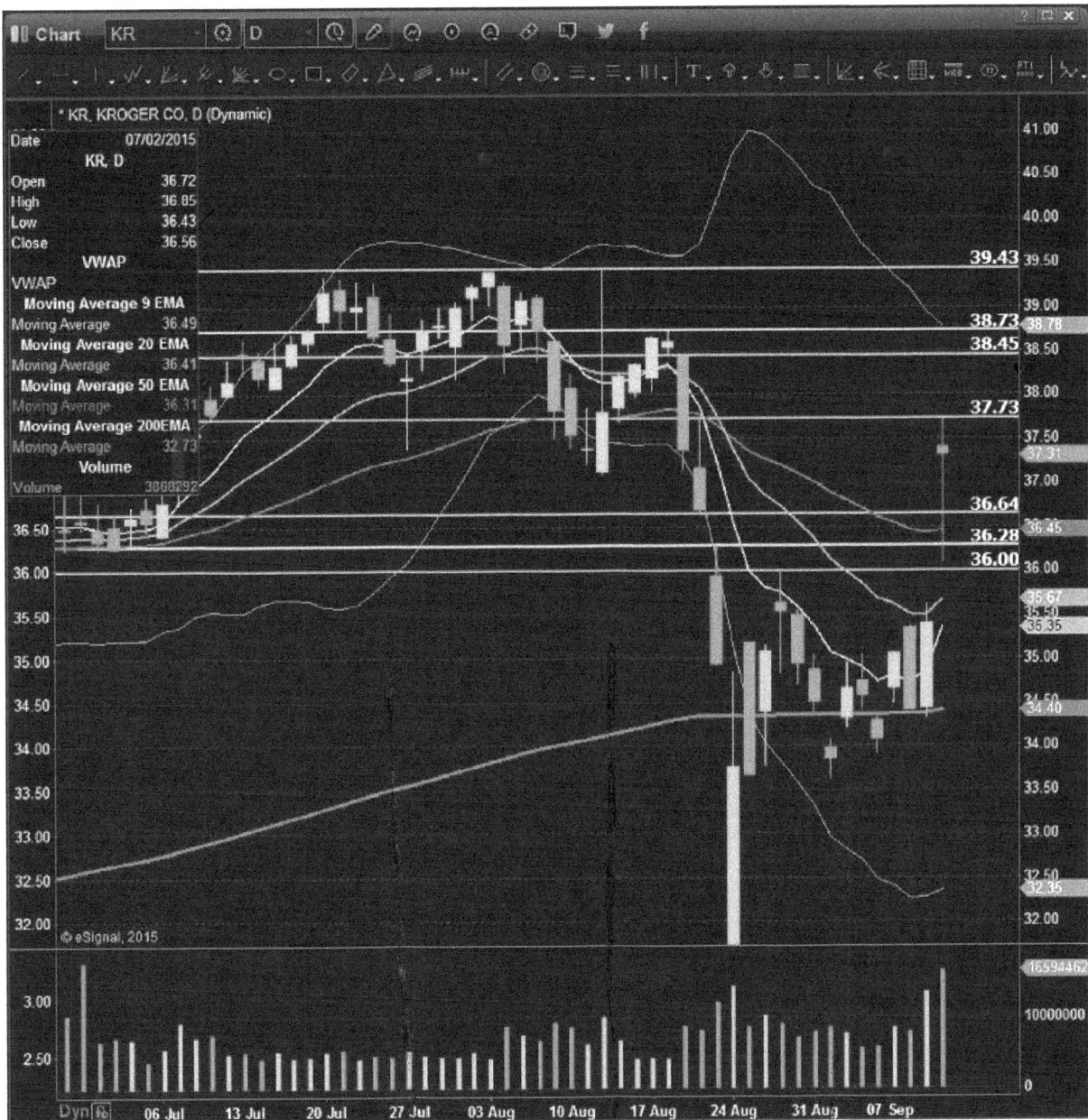

Daily Chart of Gapper - Marking out recent price levels of possible support/resistance.

When I am looking at the stocks each morning that are trading on above average volume, I like to look at the daily chart to identify nearby areas of support or resistance. When you look back for previous levels of support or resistance, you have to remember that the level is only valid if the price has not been broken since the day that high or low was made. That means if a candle two months ago had a high of $10.00, and a candle yesterday made a high of $10.10, the high of $10.00 is no longer relevant. That high was broken. If a stock is running up, I will look for the next obvious resistance point. This will typically take the form of the high or low of a candle. I will mark out each of these recent levels, so if I decide to take a day trade, I will be aware of potential levels where we might find sellers holding the price back. If there is no resistance on a chart, that gives me a sense of increased potential, but only if the catalyst is strong.

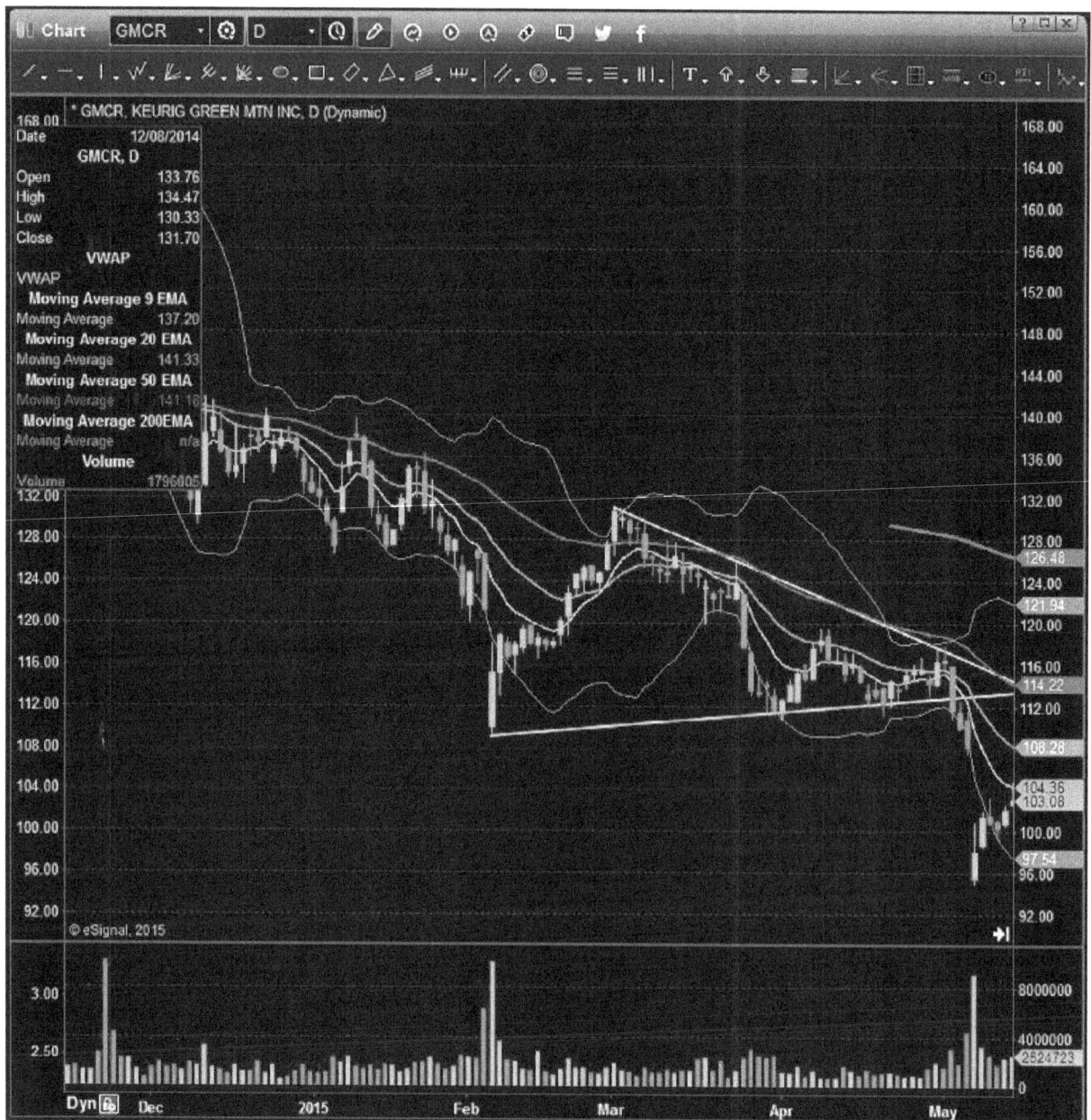

Chart of Ascending and Descending Trend Lines.

Ascending and Descending Support and Resistance Lines

In addition to horizontal support and resistance lines, we can draw both ascending and descending support and resistance lines. These lines are not always as obvious as horizontal levels. Since they are less obvious, they are also not always well respected by traders. Whenever I'm drawing trend lines on a chart, I want to draw them in what seems like the most obvious place. This means we need to see lots of candles tapping the trend line and confirming its validity. My charts typically have a lot of horizontal lines at recent support and resistance areas, with one or two ascending or descending trend lines based on the large trend of the last several months. Occasionally, I will draw a descending trend line during the formation of a pullback, or to highlight the top or bottom of a flag pattern. These types of trend lines typically span the length of just a few days of price action.

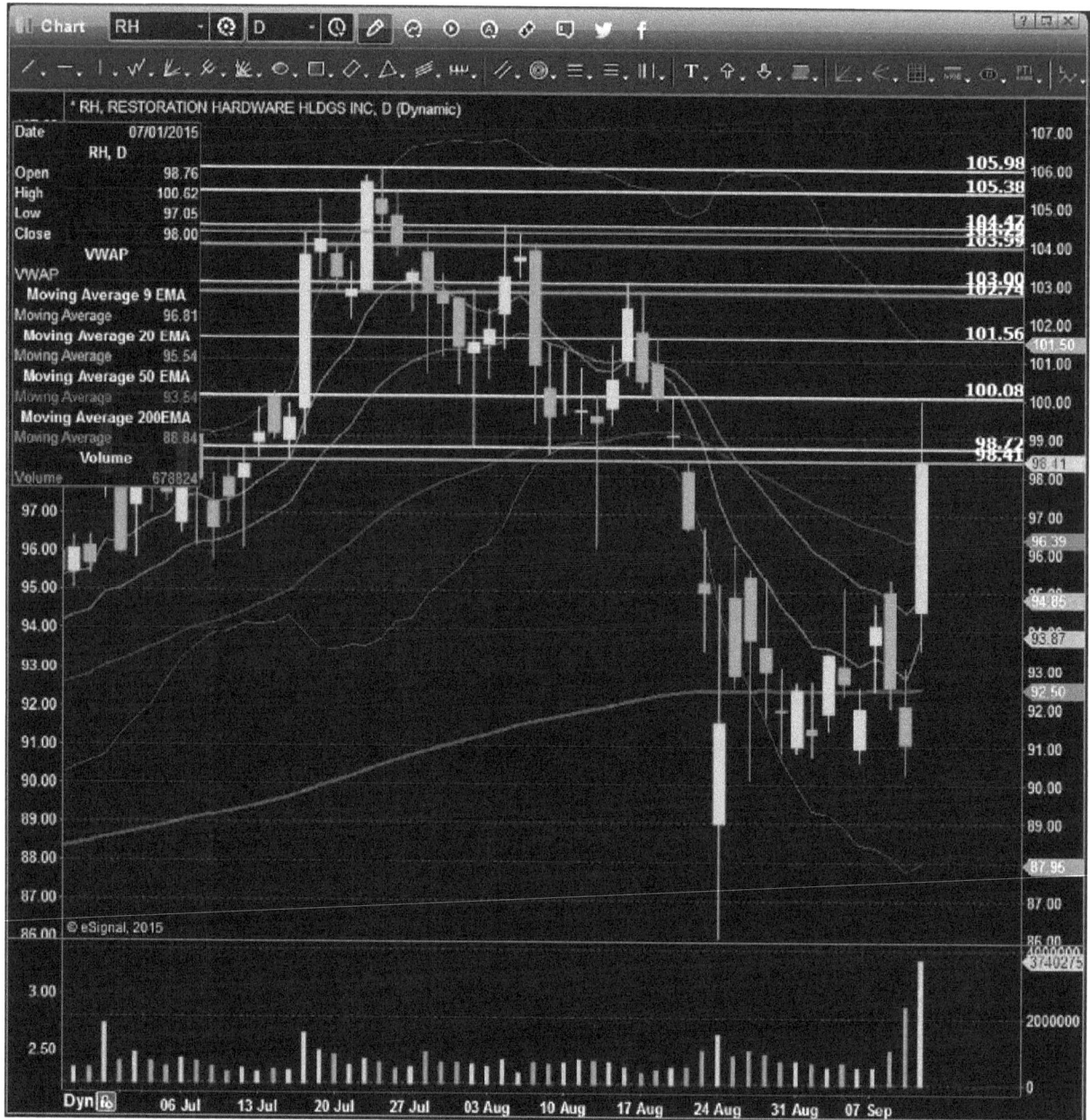

Chart of Triggers (in orange) and Resistance (in red).

Windows & Triggers

When I look at daily charts, I am looking for windows with no support and resistance. I know when the price action gets inside that window, we have breakout potential and the price can squeeze to the top or bottom of the window. It's important to note that we only want to trade stocks that have breakout potential. If a stock has the potential to move $1.00 we may only be able to capture half of the move. So if a stock doesn't have potential to make a big move it's not worth watching. These windows that we're looking for have to be extremely obvious in order to get the high relative volume needed to get a big move. Based on the strategies I trade, windows and triggers are only in play on stocks that have high relative volume due to a catalyst. For this reason, I don't spend a lot of time looking for windows and triggers on the daily charts of random stocks. I only analyze the charts of stocks that are in play each day due to news.

What is the difference between a trigger and a resistance level? Technically, a trigger is a potential resistance level, but the difference between calling it resistance and calling it a trigger is based on how much room it has until the next resistance level. A resistance level that has a large window of no resistance above it, is called a trigger. A window on a chart must be larger than the Average True Range (ATR) of the stock in order for me to consider it significant. Every stock has an average true range based on the price range of the last 14 days. If a stock has a 50 cent ATR, that means it moves on average 50 cents every day. If I was looking at the daily chart of that stock and noticed a resistance price that did not have another resistance level above it for 75 cents, I would consider it a trigger. If the price can break over that trigger, there is potential for a move up to the next level. On the other hand, if you notice a price level that has another level of resistance in 10 cents, and another level in another 10 cents, those are all little areas of resistance. There are not any triggers there because the price levels are packed too closely together. The best daily charts will have big windows and big triggers at the top and bottom of each window. The space that creates the windows can be long body candles or gaps. Those are the only two ways a window can be created on a chart.

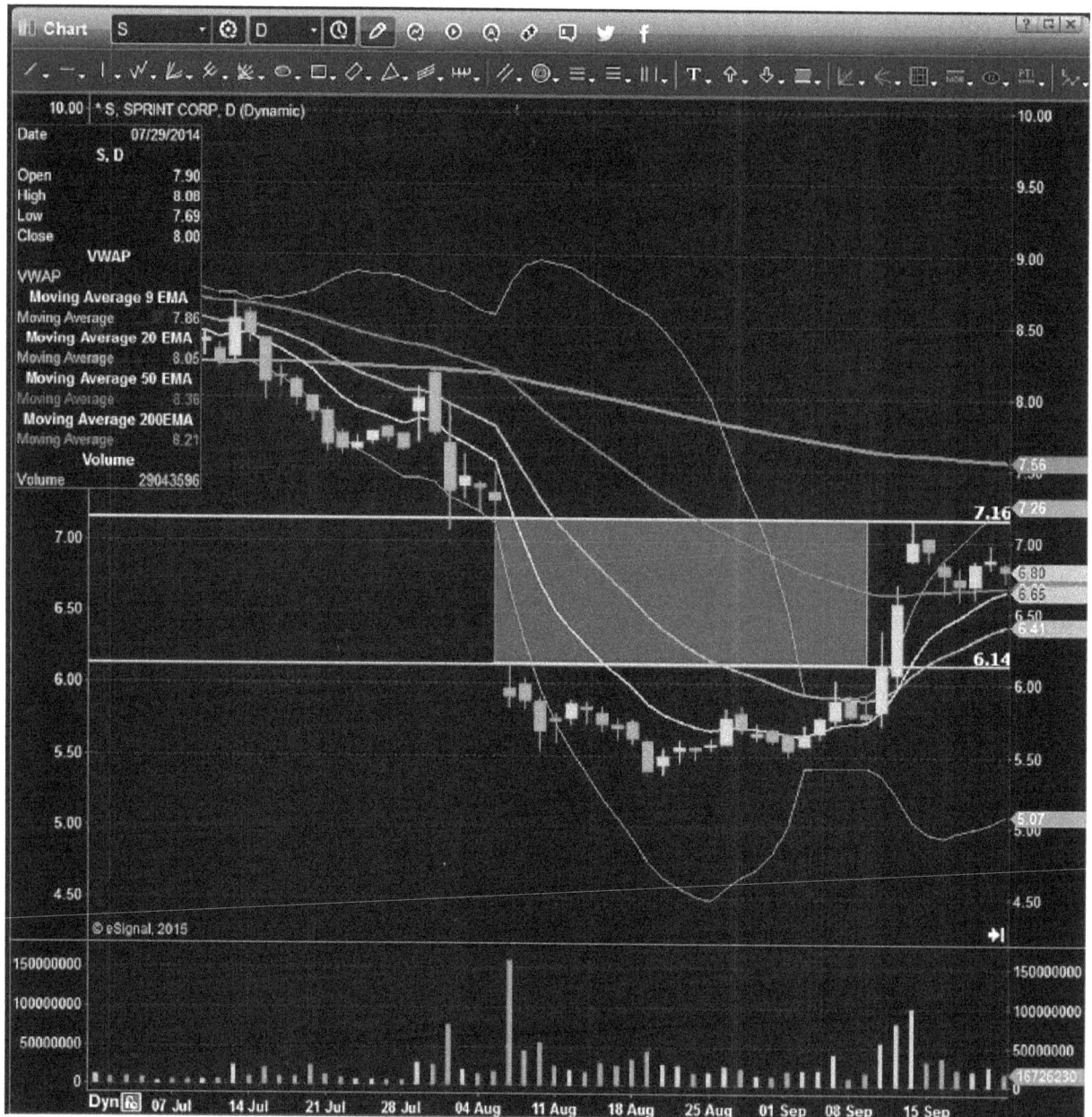

Chart of a Gap Fill. Once the price gets into the gap we have breakout potential.

Gaps

If you look at almost any chart, you will see gaps. These are the days where the stock opened much higher or lower than the previous trading day. Gap days are caused by some type of fundamental catalyst such as earnings, a press release or some other big piece of news. We know that we will usually be trading stocks on the gap days, but it is also important to understand how those large gaps can be traded in the future. When a stock has a big gap, there is a large window on the chart and those windows will typically get filled. Gap fill occurs when the price of a stock moves into a gap window present on the chart. The original gap that created the window could have occurred in the last few days, months or even years. The window remains open and valid until the price action has closed it. Since we know there is no resistance inside the window, once a stock starts moving into the window, the gap often gets filled rather quickly. In contrast to the windows created by long body candles, windows created by gaps often get more buying attention. I believe this is a result of the gap window being more obvious to retail traders than long body candle windows. Since the market is comprised of many individual traders, our collective knowledge can become a factor in the success or failure of a pattern. A simple and obvious pattern will often result in cleaner and more decisive breakouts, because more traders see the opportunity. Complex patterns may only be noticeable to the most experienced traders, which will result in fewer traders buying at the critical breakout spot and therefore, less volume. For this reason, I am a big advocate of keeping it simple. I focus on trading the most obvious windows, triggers, and patterns, because they typically work the best. Trading becomes increasingly difficult when we over complicate it. When you are preparing to take a trade, try asking yourself if the setup is obvious. I have often found myself forcing trades, or trading obscure patterns out of boredom. Those trades rarely produce big winners and instead just rack up commission costs and distract me from better opportunities.

Support and Resistance at Whole Dollars and Half Dollars

In addition to the support and resistance levels we will find from ascending or descending trend lines, windows, or gaps, we will also see support and resistance as stocks approach whole dollars and half dollars. A stock approaching levels such as $10.00, $10.50, $11.00, etc, will typically see resistance at those whole and half dollar marks. Conversely, a stock selling off may find support as it drops down to whole dollars and half dollars. Whenever possible, I try to take entries near whole dollar and half dollar marks, because I can usually set my stop on the other side of that price level. When traditional chart patterns line up with whole dollars and half dollars, it adds considerable strength to the setup. Stocks priced below $10.00, will often have more difficulty breaking through those critical levels than higher priced stocks. A break of a whole dollar such as $3.00, could be an opportunity to take a long position with a stop at $2.90 or $2.95. Stocks of all price ranges respond well to the price support and resistance of whole dollars and half dollars.

Typically, if I am in a long position and a stock is approaching a whole dollar, I begin taking profit in the .90's, before it hits resistance, and keep the remaining position with a stop at breakeven. I would expect to see prices tap the whole dollar to test the resistance level and then pullback. Sometimes, that tap becomes the high of day and the trend reverses. If I enter a position at $9.99, in anticipation of the whole dollar break, I use a tight 10 cent stop, because I am entering a stock near the highs. If prices break over the whole dollar, it is very important that it stays above the whole dollar. If prices break over the resistance level and then break back below, I will sometimes use this as an opportunity to take a short position with a 10 cent stop. Trading over and under the whole dollars and half dollars can provide the opportunity for great entries on both momentum and reversal trades. Trading around whole dollars carries a bit more risk than traditional chart patterns because the entries are often in anticipation of breakouts or reversals. For this reason, I always keep tight stops on these trades. It is important to note that trading over and under whole dollars and half dollars is only significant on stocks trading on high relative volume or trading at intraday extremes.

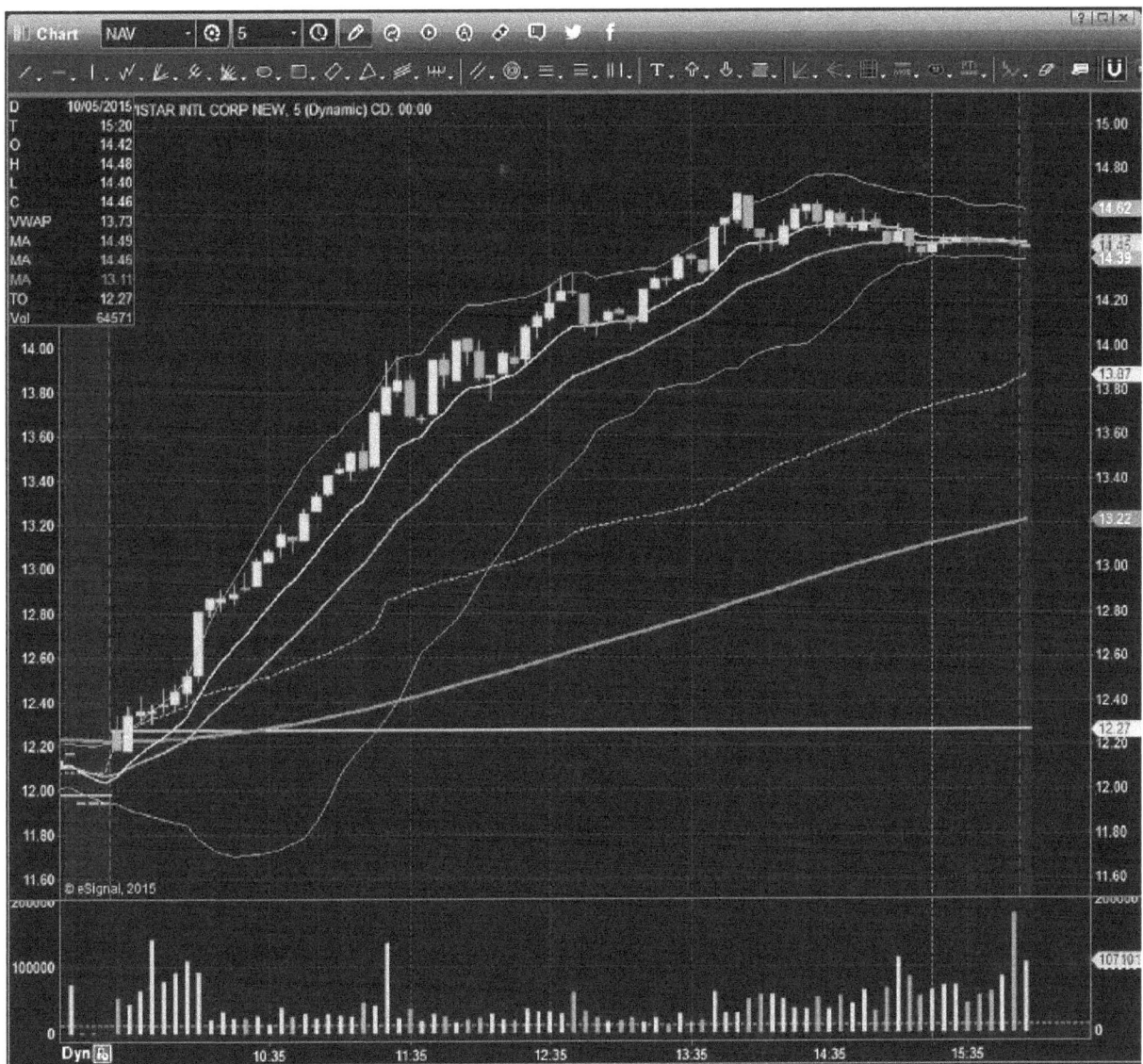

A chart showing 9 EMA support.

Moving Average Support and Resistance

Both daily charts and intraday charts respect moving averages. When a weak stock gaps up it's not uncommon for the price to open around moving average resistance. Even though the stock has gapped up, it will struggle with the daily resistance levels unless the catalyst is particularly strong. I typically look to trade stocks in the direction of the daily trend. A stock gapping up should be breaking up and away from its moving averages just as a stock gapping down should be breaking down and away from its moving averages. We can use the information of daily windows and gaps, the levels of trend line support, and the position of the moving averages to help us create our long or short bias against a stock. This becomes the basis for how we will trade the stock.

On an intraday level moving averages present one of the most significant forms of support and resistance. It's very common to see trending stocks respecting the support of moving averages. It's important to recognize this support because if we have a long bias we can use moving average pullbacks as entry opportunities. Often times these pullbacks will also take the familiar form of a bull flag. In addition to noting the importance of moving average support and resistance, it's important to be mindful of when price crosses moving averages. If the price has been respecting the 9 EMA all day long and suddenly crosses below it, there could be an opportunity for a trend reversal. We will cover the details of these trading strategies later on, but for now I'd encourage you to keep a close eye on how stocks trade around their moving averages.

CHAPTER 7

ORDER TYPES, LEVEL2, TIME & SALES, HOTKEYS

Before we get into the detailed strategies I use every day, it is important to understand how to actually buy and sell stock. There is a vast number of brokers and platforms a new trader can choose from, and there is not any single broker that is the best for everyone. Depending on your needs as a trader, different brokers may suit you better than others. We will focus on the features required for day trading and then discuss the details of entering and exiting positions using Level2, time and sales, and hotkeys.

Not All Brokers Are The Same

We will begin by first comparing different types of brokers. Most day traders use desktop brokerage applications that connect directly to their broker, and to the market exchanges. Day traders require two important features from their broker, fast executions and competitive commissions. Remember that the best prices are worthless if the broker does not offer fast executions or a reliable trading platform.

Part-time traders typically use full-service brokers that offer mutual funds, research tools, automatic bill pay from your brokerage account, ATM/debit card and checkbooks. This type of broker is extremely convenient, but you typically pay for that convenience with higher commissions. Every time you place a trade, your broker will charge a commission. Some brokers charge commissions based on the number of shares you trade, while most charge simply per order. Full service brokers have commissions ranging from $9.95 to 19.95 per trade. If you place one order to buy, and one order to sell, you get charged for two orders. Since day traders often trade ten or more times a day, we need to find a broker that will provide a better commission structure based on our increased trading activity.

Full service brokers do not cater to day traders. Instead, they cater to part-time investors looking to take a few positions and manage their own retirement accounts. Those types of customers make up the bulk of their business. Full service brokers offer platforms that tend to run slower, because they offer a lot of features for research and analysis. This lag time can be a real burden for a day trader. Day traders typical prefer a bare bones platform that runs fast and reliably. Lastly, most full service brokers have slower execution speeds, because they do not allow the customers to choose which electronic communication network (ECN) will be used to send orders to the exchange. As a part-time trader, you truly do not have to worry about ECN routing, but as an active day trader, you will notice that some routes are faster than others. Often the "in house" ECN route from full service firms is far slower than ECN routes most day traders use. The simple conclusion is, that subpar execution speed is unacceptable for day trading.

Professional day traders seek out brokers that offer commissions of $4.95 per trade or less, and provide direct access routing. At Warrior Trading, we have close relationships with several brokers that cater to day traders. These brokers offer our students discounted commissions of $2.00 per trade for direct access routing. Direct access routing means you can choose which ECN route you will send your orders through. This gives you more control over your trading results. It is also important to highlight the fact that you can possess all the textbook knowledge and emotional conditioning to be a great trader, but lack the proper tools.

Order Types (Limit, Market, Stops)

There are several different order types available to traders. The most popular are Market Orders, Limit Orders and Stop Orders. We will review these order types and discuss the techniques I use while day trading.

A market order requires two pieces of information. The stock you want to buy, and the number of shares you want to buy. You provide that information, press the buy button, and your broker will get you the shares and process the order. The risk with a market order, is, that you have not stipulated a price. In volatile markets, sending a market order can result in a high degree of slippage (the difference in price you thought you would pay versus the price you actually paid). A market order will give you shares at the current market price at the moment your order is processed. Market orders may be suitable for part-time traders that are taking small positions with the intention of holding for several days, weeks or months. However, for day traders navigating fast moving markets, they carry an unacceptable level of risk.

A limit order, in contrast to a market order, requires three pieces of information. The stock you want to buy, the number of shares you want to buy, and the maximum price you are willing to pay. Limit orders, once sent, will give you as many shares as possible within the price you have set. Sometimes the order will come back partially filled, because the price of the stock moved up too quickly. Most times, however, you will get the full order at the current market price. I use limit orders for all my trades. To ensure that I get filled with my full position, I use what is called an offset. If I want to buy a stock at $5.00, I use a limit order of $5.05. The 5 cent offset means the broker can try to find me shares up to $5.05, but no higher. I use limit orders with a 5 cent offset whenever I'm entering or exiting trades.

The third order type is called a Stop Order. A stop order requires three pieces of information. The stock you want to sell, the number of shares you want to sell at, and the trigger price that should execute the order.

A stop order is an order you place that will sit as an active and pending order until a trigger price is hit. If you are holding a position of 1,000 shares, and the current price is $5.10, you could set a stop order of $4.99. When the price crosses $4.99, your order will automatically get sent, selling your shares. There are two types of stops, Market Stops and Limit Stops. A market stop will send the order as a market order, while stops limits send the order as a limit order. Stop orders can be used to exit long or short positions, or they can be used to initiate new positions. A buy stop is an order you set to buy shares of a stock when the price crosses a certain level. Many traders will set buy stop orders at a critical breakout spot, so they do not have to worry about missing the breakout because they got distracted. The important thing to remember about this type of stop order is, that using a stop limit will be important in case the market spikes dramatically at the breakout spot. You would not want to get filled at the top of that spike on a market order.

Level2 and Time & Sales Window by Lightspeed.

Level2

Once you have setup an account with the broker you feel will be a good fit for your needs, you should be able to pull up a few different tools from inside the platform. You will need to pull up a Market Depth (Level2) window, a Time and Sales window, and an Order Entry window. With some brokers, all three tools are included in one window, while others have separate windows for each tool. When you are looking at the Market Depth window, you will first see the Level1 prices on top. Level1 is the first level of the market, this is the simple bid and ask price, also known as the National Best Bid and Best Offer (NBBO). The bid price is always on the left, and the ask price is always on the right. The bid is the price where there are buyers looking to purchase shares and the ask is the price where there are sellers looking to sell shares. A Level1 quote, which is what many part-time traders will use to place their orders, shows you the current bid and ask prices. However, Level1 is only the very surface of the market. As day traders, we want to know the Market Depth. The Market Depth, also called Level2, is two columns of price with the bid on the left and the ask on the right. Level2 shows us the actual number of buyers and sellers on both the bid and the ask. This can give us a sense of the sentiment of a stock by telling us if there are more buyers or sellers. A typical Level1 quote would not give you that depth of information.

SELLAS Life Sciences Group, Inc. ⚙ – ▢ ✕

▼ SLS Ⓛ 25%

TIER SM1		CLOSE 3.45		LAST 9.90	
HI 10.00		OPEN 5.60		VOL 10,085.0	
LO 5.40		CHG +6.45		CHG % +186.95%	

Bid Mkt	Bid	Size	Ask Mkt	Ask	Size	Q/R	Price	Sz
NSDQ*	9.90	57	NSDQ	9.99	10	Q	9.90	1
ARCA	9.85	1	EDGX*	10.00	252	Q	9.90	4
EDGX	9.84	10	ARCA	10.00	22	Q	9.90	20
BATY	9.71	5	IMCC	10.39	1	Q	9.92	1
BATS	9.60	1	LULD	10.39	1	R	9.99	1
PHLX	9.53	2	EDGA	10.47	2	Q	9.92	1
IMCC	9.47	1	ETMM	10.64	1	R	9.95	7
EDGA	9.23	1	SUFI	10.64	1	Q	9.95	1
SSUS	9.23	1	BATS	10.68	2	Q	9.95	2
ETMM	9.16	1	BATY	10.68	2	Q	9.90	19
SUFI	9.16	1	BOSX	10.68	2	R	9.90	2
BOSX	9.01	1	PHLX	10.68	2	R	9.90	1
						R	9.91	1
						R	9.95	5
						R	9.95	12

Order Entry 3 : SLS ⚙ – ▢ ✕

Symbol	Shares	Price	Market
SLS	2500	9.73	BATS

Type	Visible		TIF
Limit	2500	0.00	DAY

	Inside Bid	Inside Ask	
Sell	9.90	9.99	Buy

Image showing a heavy seller (25,200 shares) sitting at 10.00, just above the current best ask price. Image from Lightspeed.

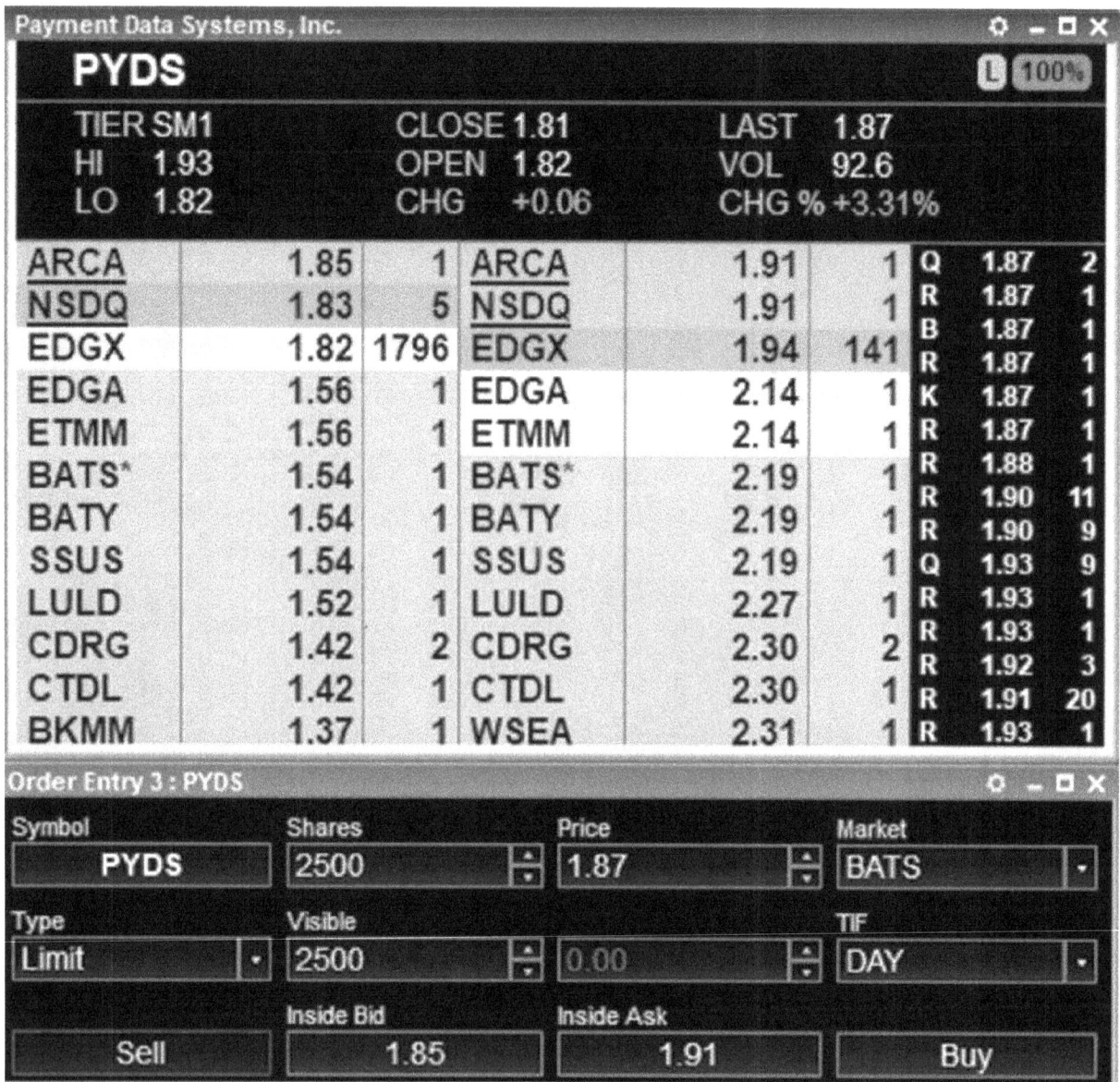

Image showing a large buyer (179,600 shares) sitting at 1.82, just below the current best bid price. Image from Lightspeed.

In addition to seeing the number of buyers and sellers at the current bid and ask, we can also see how many buyers are lined up below the current price, and how many sellers are lined up above the current price. If for instance we see a 121,300 share seller sitting at the ask price, we may recognize that seller as a form of resistance. We could decide, based on that information, that this may not be a safe place to enter the trade. Alternatively, if we see a big buyer sitting at the bid price we may feel confident there is somebody supporting the price for a long entry. Large orders on the Level2 can give insight into levels of price support and resistance. Price support and resistance on the Level2 will be most valuable when it lines up with support and resistance on the chart. When they do not line up, it is possible that there is simply a big buyer or seller sitting on the stock. It is also possible that the order is placed there intentionally, to give traders a false sense of confidence. This is called spoofing. Traders that are spoofing will put out large orders with the intention of manipulating the market, and never actually allow the order to get executed. If the current trading price begins to move close to their large order, they will cancel the order and move it down a few more cents. Spoofing is an illegal form of market manipulation. Since manipulation does exist using Level2, I only start looking at Level2 once I have found a good chart pattern.

I find my setups by looking through stock scanners and looking through charts. However, once I am ready to take the trade, I am only looking at the Level2. I already know the price I want to buy at, and where my stop price is. So, all I need to see is what the Level2 can tell me about market sentiment. Is there a heavy seller sitting right where I want to buy? If that is the case, I will wait for those shares to get bought up, and just before they are gone, I will send my order and jump into the market. If I am in a trade and I suddenly see a large buyer come in and prop up the price, I will recognize that as a new level of support. Regardless of the support level I see on the chart, the buyer on the Level2 has stepped up to provide another visual level of support. Since we are trading simultaneously with many other traders, we can all recognize the subtle cues given on the Level2, and typically will react similarly.

Image showing various routes available. This is the benefit of

Direct Access Routing. Image from Lightspeed.

As you can probably imagine, the Level2 moves around very quickly. Orders are constantly flowing through, prices are moving, and learning to read the Level2 while it is moving can take some time. One of the things you will notice on the Level2 is, that each row will represent a price, a number of shares and the ECN that is holding those shares. If for instance, we see that ARCA (an ECN) has 1,000 shares at $5.00, we could use direct access routing to try to quickly buy those shares directly from ARCA. If we send the same order through the ECN route NYSE or EDGX, they would both try to get the same shares from ARCA, but they might be just a few milliseconds slower. The Level2 is like an island where all the ECN's come together. They communicate with each other, and buy and sell from each other. As traders, we will learn to recognize that on some stocks, a certain ECN is more dominant than others. When that is the case, I could choose to route directly to the ECN that is displayed as holding shares. Remember, that in regard to execution times, the difference between different ECN's may be only milliseconds. The difference between using a full service "in house" route versus a direct access ECN could be several seconds. If you choose to always use the same ECN with a direct access broker, you probably will not notice any loss in execution speed, especially on stocks with above average relative volume. I generally find it easier to always use the same ECN, preferably ARCA or BATS.

Time and Sales

To the right of my Level2 window, I have a time and sales window. The time and sales window will show each transaction that passes through. While the Level2 is jumping around giving you the latest quotes, it does not actually show orders that are placed. The time and sales window will show you the number of shares, the time, the price and the route where the trade was executed. I watch the time and sales and Level2 closely while I am preparing to take a trade and while I am holding a position. If for example I see a heavy seller sitting on the ask, I will look to the time and sales to start seeing orders flowing through, indicating the shares are being purchased. If I see large blocks of 5,000 share orders going through time and sales, that may give me increased confidence that traders are taking large positions for the breakout. Alternatively, if I enter a trade and suddenly the time and sales comes to a stop, and the market stops moving, I may begin to think I mistimed my entry and should sell breakeven or for a small loss. Time and sales will show the volume that is passing through in a very visual sense. When there are a ton of orders executing from other traders, the time and sales window will be flashing as they pass through. This is what we want to see for strong momentum stocks breaking out.

Twitter, Inc. Common Stock

▲ TWTR   E 25%

TIER NY1		CLOSE 29.01		LAST 28.35	
HI 28.77		OPEN 28.37		VOL 15,598.8	
LO 27.75		CHG -0.66		CHG % -2.27%	

NSDQ	28.34	7	NSDQ	28.35	9	R 28.35	1
BATS	28.34	7	EDGX	28.35	9	J 28.34	1
EDGX	28.34	6	BATS	28.35	5	Q 28.34	1
BATY*	28.34	5	NYSE	28.35	4	Z 28.34	1
ARCA	28.34	4	ARCA	28.36	2	N 28.34	7
BOSX	28.34	3	PHLX	28.36	1	J 28.34	1
EDGA	28.34	2	BATY*	28.37	2	R 28.34	1
IEXG	28.34	1	BOSX	28.37	2	R 28.33	20
NYSE	28.34	16	AMEX	28.37	1	R 28.34	1
AMEX	28.34	1	EDGA	28.60	2	R 28.34	1
PHLX	28.33	1	SUNT	28.89	1	R 28.34	1
SUNT	27.76	1	IEXG	28.91	1	Q 28.33	1
						N 28.33	3
						Z 28.33	1

Order Entry 3 : TWTR

Symbol	Shares	Price	Market
TWTR	2500	28.33	BATS

Type	Visible		TIF
Limit	2500	0.00	DAY

Sell	Inside Bid 28.34	Inside Ask 28.35	Buy

I prepare trades pre-market by entering the share size, the price, and choosing the route. All I need to do is press the BUY or SELL buttons when the market opens. Image from Lightspeed.

Entering Trades

When I am entering trades, I usually have a few minutes to think about my entry and my stop loss. Most trades will be based on a pre-market pattern, or will be based on a midday pattern that has been forming for several minutes or hours. This is a good time to note that I rarely trade pre-market or after hours. I prefer to focus my trading during regular market hours because that's when we see the most volume. With that said, I do keep a close eye on any patterns or support and resistance levels that were formed pre-market. During the pre-market session I typically prepare my orders manually in the order entry window so when the market opens at 9:30 I'm ready to trade. The order entry window is where I enter the price, add the 5 cent offset for the limit order, choose the share size and choose the ECN route. I always have at least four order entry windows up at any given time. This means I can have four different orders ready to send. All I need to do is click the buy or sell button. Once I am in the trade, I begin to use hotkeys to manage my position.

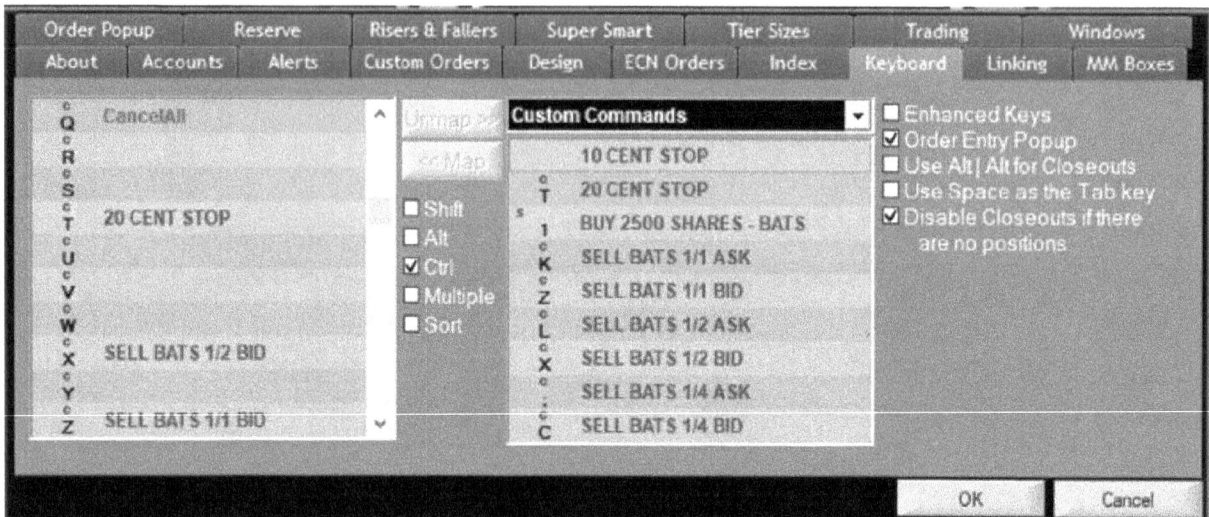

Image of my Hot Key settings from Lightspeed.

Hot Keys

Some of the trading strategies I use, require high speed trading. As we know the market can be irrationally strong. We have seen stocks run over 100%, in a matter of minutes, especially at the market open. In order to capitalize on these moves in the market, it is important to use a broker that allows direct access routing and hot keys. Hot keys are key commands that can be programmed to automatically send orders with the touch of a key. Professional day traders will use hot keys to enter trades, exit trades, place stop orders and cancel orders. Having all of our possible trade combinations at our fingertips can allow for high speed trading. Midday trades do not usually require the use of hotkeys since they are often slower than trades at the open. The market trades on the highest volume consistently in the first hour of trading. This is when we have the most volatility in the market. My Gap and Go strategy and morning Momentum Strategy require the use of hotkeys, to maximize profit and minimize losses. Typically, I will enter these trades using manually entered buy or short orders, and then start using the hot keys to manage my position, including placing stop orders and partial profit taking orders.

My favorite hotkey is the command to sell half my position on the bid price (Control+X) or on the ask price (Control+L). The computer system will automatically calculate what half of my position equals, in number shares. The computer will also calculate the current bid and ask price and place my order at the price I ask. The huge advantage of these hotkeys is that when a stock suddenly spikes up 50 cents, I can press my hotkey to sell my full position on the bid (Control+Z) without having to type in the new bid price or my number of shares. In the time it takes to type, the price could come right back down. So, the use of hot keys eliminates the delay of manual entry. The volatility at the open can allow for huge profits if you can trade it properly, but can also result in large losses if you fail to act quickly. In addition to using hotkeys for selling partial and full positions on the bid or ask, I also have hotkeys for setting automatic stops. I have a hotkey that I can press that will set a stop at my average cost or at breakeven (Control+B). I also have hotkeys I can press to set a stop loss for my full position -11 cents (Control+1), -21 cents (Control+2) or -31 cents (Control+3) away from the last price traded.

When you are first using hotkeys, it is a good idea to keep your order confirmation windows turned on. It is very common to make some mistakes when you are getting used to them. I have stickers on my keyboard to help me keep track of the different key combinations.

When I was learning to use hotkeys, I would sit with my computer turned off at night, and practiced pressing the right buttons. It takes some time, but eventually it will become second nature. Another important reminder is that you always use a hardwired keyboard that is plugged into your computer. Wireless keyboards can begin to lose battery power can send repeat keystrokes, errant keystrokes and can fail to send orders at all. This could result in accidentally repeatedly buying shares of a stock until your buying power has been maxed out. Hotkeys are an amazing tool, but have to be used with caution to prevent errors. Trading is difficult enough without making technical errors with hotkeys.

CHAPTER 8

TREND (MOMENTUM) TRADING STRATEGIES

Now that you have a solid understanding of support and resistance, basic chart settings, and how to select stocks worth trading, I want to discuss finding your entry. This is where the rubber meets the road. We are going to talk about chart patterns and setups, as well as opportunities to enter the right type of stock while managing risk and keeping losses minimal. I define a chart setup as having a safe opportunity to get into a strong stock. You may find that some of the patterns we review seem a bit obscure, but I assure you that the longer you look at charts, the more obvious they will become. When we are trading, we always want to refer back to taking setups that are obvious, because that means more people will be likely to buy at the same breakout spots. The most important thing to remember about momentum trading is that entering close to support will always give you the lowest risk and the highest reward potential. This typically means buying near moving average support or at the bottom of a bull flag pullback. While buying stocks near high of day can work in strong markets, it is also a higher risk strategy. Instead, we will focus on pullback entries that occur during the formation of a chart pattern commonly known as a flag.

Anytime you are considering taking a trade, you need to make sure you can justify the risk. That means you need to understand what the risk actually is. My favorite patterns all have well defined levels of support that we use as the max loss price. If the stock breaks below that support level, we take the loss and move on. I will base my position size on the distance between my entry and the stop and how much money I am willing to risk in the trade. Once I have established my risk, my profit target needs to be my risk multiplied by two. That will give me the 2:1 profit loss that is critical for long term success as a trader. We have already discussed the added value of strong daily charts with lots of triggers and windows, and the importance of a good intraday catalyst. In this chapter, we will be applying the chart patterns only to the strong stocks we consider worthy of trading. Chart patterns on weak stocks are irrelevant to us.

My favorite strategies are momentum trading strategies to the long side. I love finding a stock during the pre-market session that has a great catalyst with a lot of windows on the daily chart. We have seen some incredible moves from momentum names over the years. One of the biggest in recent memory was from a stock that opened at $18.00, and hit a high of just over $55.00, within 60 minutes of trading. When stocks make those types of intraday moves, it is a reminder to never underestimate the strength of the market. As a momentum trader, I am often buying stocks that have already made a big move. As an investor, it would not make a lot of sense to buy a stock that just moved up 5-10%, but as a day trader, we know we can manage our risk based on the intraday support level and try to ride the trend for another 5-10%. It is commonplace for stocks under $10 to make 50% intraday moves when a catalyst or high relative volume is present.

For all my trading strategies, I use Limit Orders to enter and exit my positions. I buy at the Ask price and usually try to sell at the Ask price as well. I am actively trading using the Level2 (market depth) window in my brokerage account. Understanding Level2 is very important for day traders, and especially when using a fast paced strategy like the Gap and Go Strategy. As we review the strategies below, you will notice me discussing the technique of selling half (scaling out) and adjusting my stops to breakeven. One of the reasons I have a high percentage of success is because as soon as I hit my first profit target, I take a little off the table and adjust my stop loss to breakeven. If I end up getting stopped out of the trade, I will still walk away from the trade with a small profit. If the stock continues to run, I can let it ride knowing that I have already locked up a winner and anything else is going to be icing on the cake. It is important to keep at least a small position in the trade until I get stopped out by an exit indicator. This confirms that I traded the stock from start to finish without exiting too soon, and it allows me to have some really big winners. With respect to losses, it is even more important to cap all of your losses at the predetermined max loss. As soon as I enter a trade, I know the price where I will stop out for a loss. Remember, a gambler thinks about profits, but a trader things about risk (loss). We have to always return to our foundation as risk managers when we are trading.

Momentum Trading Strategy

Remember one of the first things I said, was that as day traders, we are hunters of volume. Momentum stocks are driven by volume. The Momentum Strategy setups include Bull Flags, Bear Flags, Flat Top Breakouts, Flat Bottom Breakdowns, Moving Average Pullbacks, and Parabolic Movers. Momentum can be traded both to the long side and the short side. The most volatile momentum stocks will almost always have low floats. I consider a low float stock as one that has under 50 million shares. The best low float runners usually have a float of under 10 million shares. These stocks have an extremely limited supply of shares to trade. Under the right circumstances, a high level of demand can create a powerful squeeze where a stock will surge 100% in a matter of minutes. This type of move could never happen on a stock with a 100 million share float. By recognizing the float, you can make a determination of the potential for a trade. Understanding potential is important because it helps us justify the risk to take the trade in the first place. When we look for profit targets on momentum trades, they will often be based on the daily chart levels of resistance, but they are also going to be influenced by the float, the catalyst and the level of volume. Low float stocks that are former runners will always have more potential than a heavy float stock.

I begin each day by running my stock scanners to find stocks that are surging up pre-market. These stocks are already trading on heavy pre-market volume, due to a catalyst of some type. I build a watch list of four to six of these stocks. I continue to run momentum stock scanners during the day to look for new ideas. The scanners I run during the day look for stocks hitting a new high of day on above average relative volume. All of the stocks hitting the scanner have potential, but it is the job of the trader to find the best opportunities.

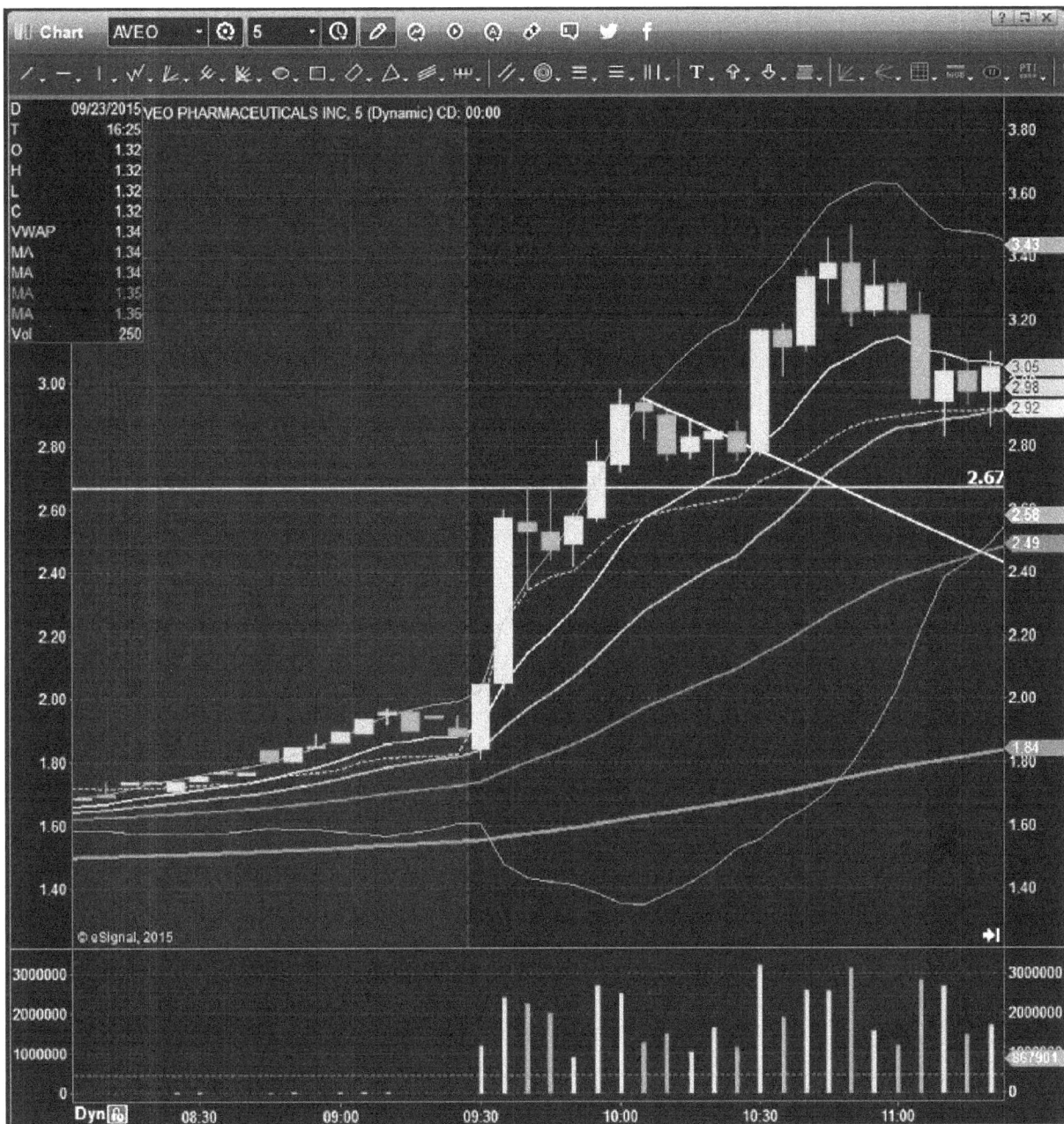

Chart showing the value of the first and second pullbacks to moving average support in the form of Bull Flags.

Buying the First and Second Pullbacks

Every time a momentum stock makes a fresh breakout, I will look to trade the breakout as well as potentially trade the first and second pullback. These pullbacks can take the form of either a bull flag, a flat top breakout or a moving average retracement. The best pullbacks are a bull flag that touch the 9 EMA. Each of these patterns will be discussed in detail below. It is important to understand the reason stocks respond well to the first and second pullbacks. It's because traders who miss the first breakout, will often seek to buy the first pullback, and some traders who missed the first pullback will trade the second pullback, especially if the stock is showing extreme strength. Again, we can confirm there is strength if extremely high relative volume is present. Beyond the second pullback, it becomes much riskier to take entries unless the stock goes through a period of consolidation. But with that said, if a stock appears to be irrationally strong, which sometimes they are, I may continue to trade beyond the second pullback. In these cases, I will use smaller position sizes to prevent giving back profit from the first trades. After a long period of consolidation, if the stock makes a fresh breakout, we can again trade that breakout and the first and second pullbacks. We look for pullbacks on both the five minute chart and the one minute chart.

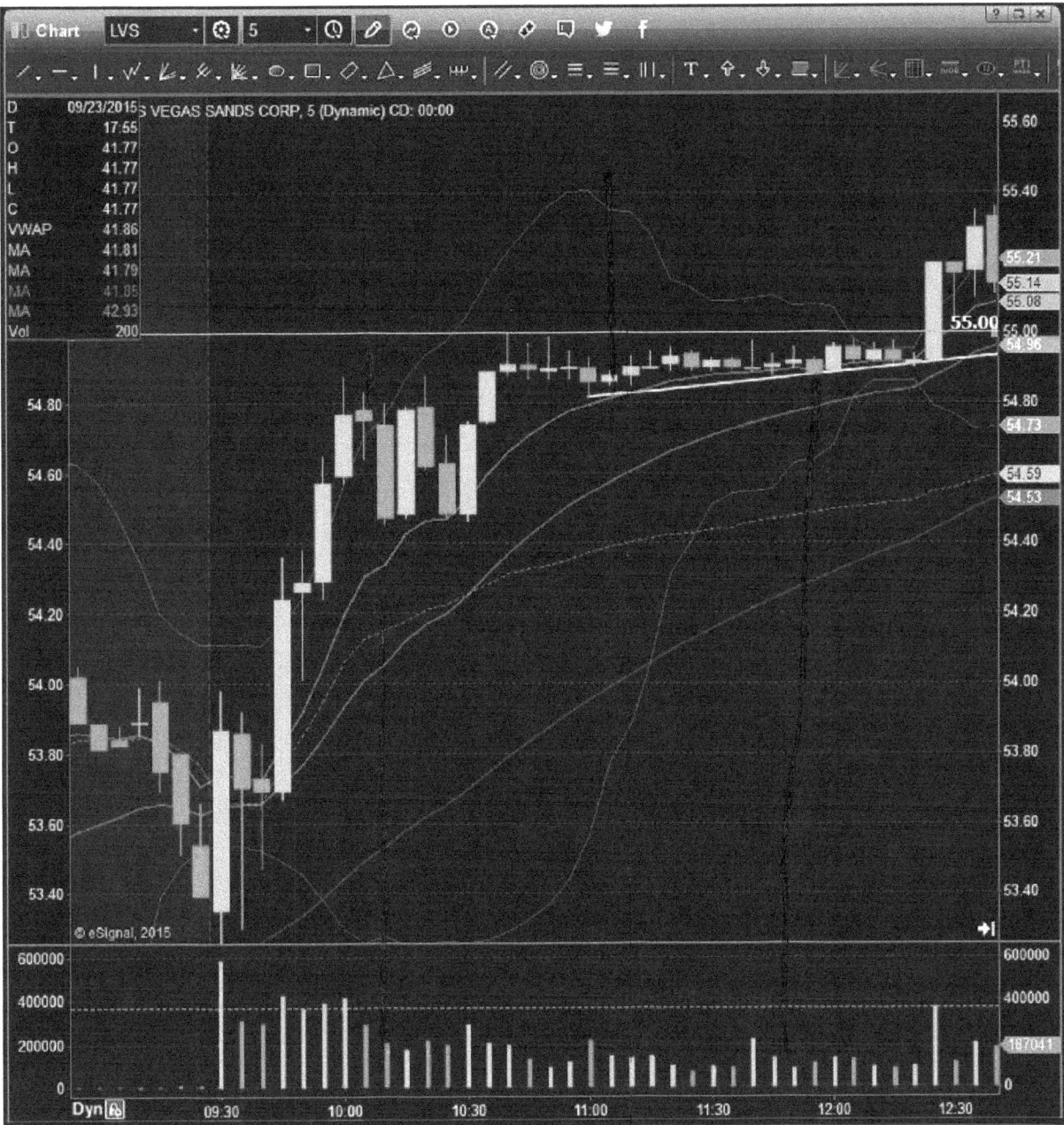

Chart of Flat Top Breakout Pattern. This Flat Top Breakout took hours to form.

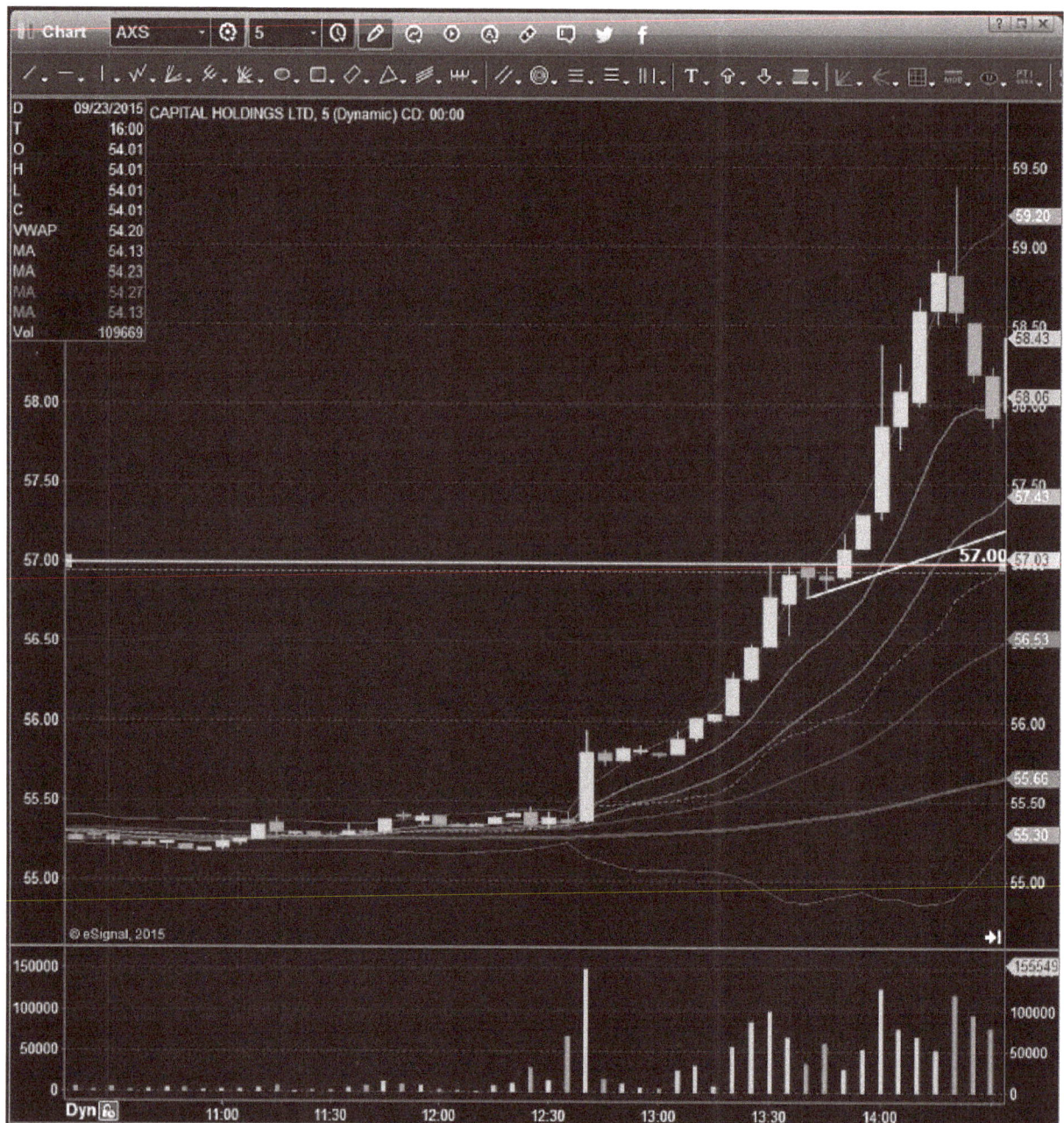

Chart of Flat Top Breakout Pattern. This flat top breakout took only a few minutes to form and did not have time to pull back to the moving average.

Flat Top Breakouts (ascending wedge)

We will start with my favorite pattern, the flat top breakout. I love flat top breakouts because they are extremely bullish and leave little room for guessing the proper breakout spot. A flat top breakout can occur on any time frame, but they are typically the strongest on the five minute chart. A flat top breakout pattern requires a stock to have made a strong move up in the last few hours, typically 4% or more. After the strong move, instead of pulling back or selling off, the stock trades sideways just below a resistance level. The period of consolidation while the flat top is forming can be as short as three to five minutes, or as long as several hours. The best flat top breakout patterns will be consolidating below a whole dollar or a half dollar level. We know stocks often find resistance around these price levels, so consolidation in that area is ideal. It is important that during the period of consolidation, the stock continues to make slightly higher lows, without it making higher highs. This forms an ascending support level. When I enter a flat top breakout pattern, my stop is just below the ascending support trend line. When the price finally breaks over the resistance point, we expect an immediate surge in volume. The volume spike confirms that thousands of other traders were watching the pattern and waiting for the breakout before buying their shares. It is not uncommon for the price to retest the breakout price shortly after the breakout. This is a retest of that level previous support level. If the level holds, prior resistance has become support and we should see a continued rally.

If a flat top breakout setup is forming, I will quickly look at the daily chart to see if we have any windows or triggers nearby. If a flat top breakout has been consolidating for several hours, it is unlikely I will see it on my stock scanners. This is because it will not be hitting high of day. I would typically only notice these long consolidation setups if I was already watching the stock, because it had high relative volume. Remember that flat top breakout patterns should only be traded on stocks with high relative volume. When I am trading flat top breakouts, I typically buy right at the apex point. The apex point is the highest price of the flat top and is the resistance price. This price, to the penny, is the breakout price. When the price breaks that level, we expect a quick surge of buying and short covering. I watch the Level2 as the stock approaches the breakout price with my order, ready to buy just before the break. If I start to see a surge in buying volume passing through the time and sales, and I see seller's sitting on the Ask and getting bought up, I will jump in with a half sized order. Buying a flat top breakout means buying a stock at the high of day. This is a bit risky, which is why I start with half size. My stop will be the ascending support line at the bottom of the wedge. If the stock fails to breakout on the first try, I will hold unless my stop gets taken out. If the stock succeeds to break over the flat top, but then immediately drops back down below the breakout price, I will sell for a loss before my stop has been touched. If the stock surges up, I will sell half my position once I have achieved a profit equal to my risk. I then adjust my stop to breakeven and hold the remaining position until I get stopped out by an exit indicator.

If I am confident in the breakout, I may add to my position during the first or second pullback after the breakout has taken place. Any traders who missed the initial breakout will use the first and second pullbacks as their buying opportunities. This is why the first and second pullbacks are often brought up on strong momentum stocks that are breaking out. If I have already sold half my position for a profit, I will add back the shares I sold at the breakout point of the pullback. I will then adjust my stop to the low of the pullback which will leave me with a profitable trade, even if I get stopped out. The first and second pullback will take place on the one minute chart, and can take the form of a bull flag or a even a flat top breakout. It is possible to be trading a flat top breakout on the five minute chart, and also trade a bull flag or flat top breakout on the one minute chart.

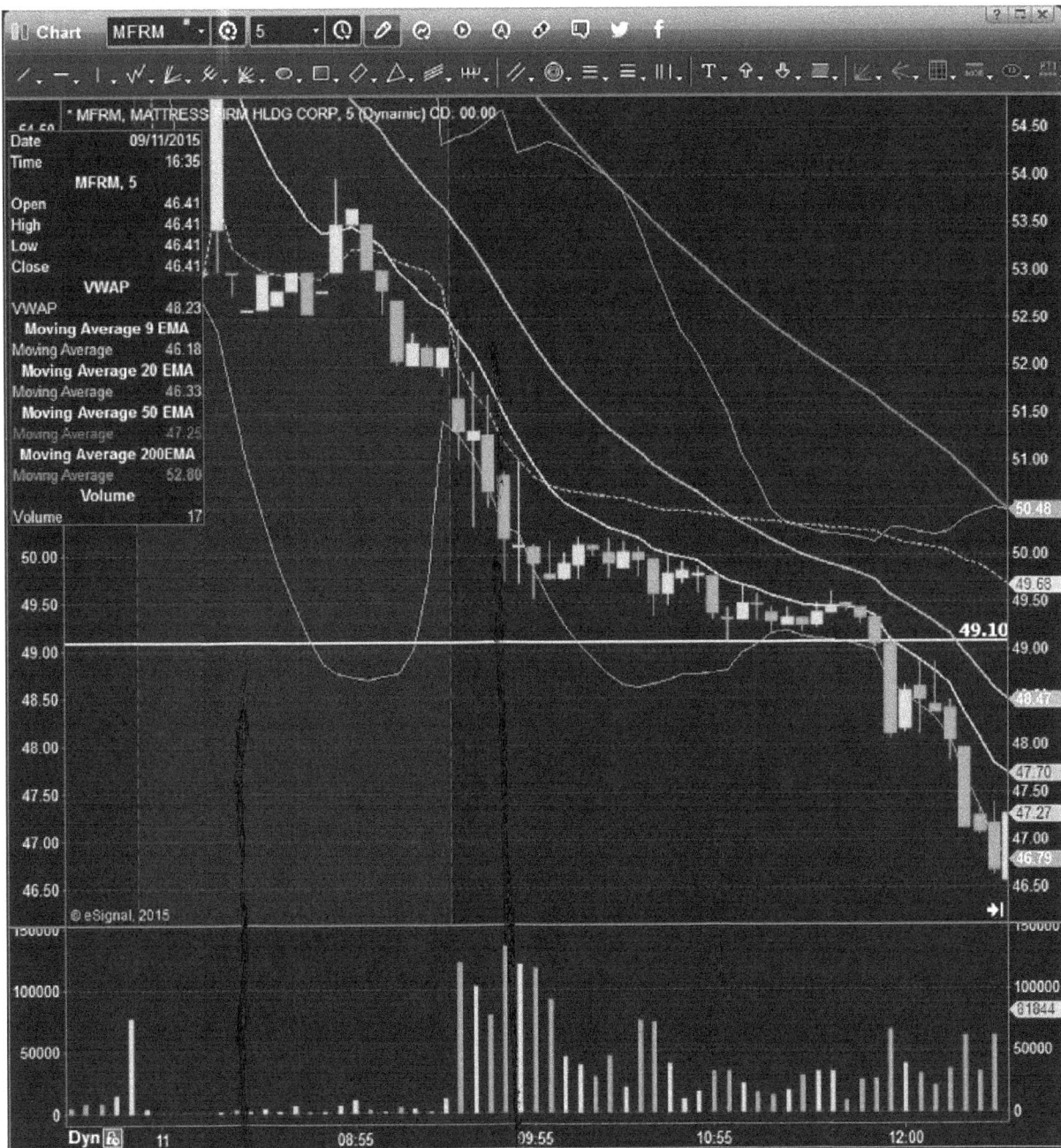

Chart of Flat Bottom Breakdown.

Flat Bottom Breakdowns

The inverse to the flat top breakout is the flat bottom breakdown. When a stock is very weak and consolidating near the lows, just above a critical support level, we have the same opportunity as a flat top breakout. There is the potential for a quick profit with a low risk entry.

As with any other setup, we want to do our due diligence and review the catalyst in play, search the daily chart for support/resistance areas, and make sure we can achieve at least a 2:1 profit loss ratio. We base this on the first profit target and the distance from a logical stop

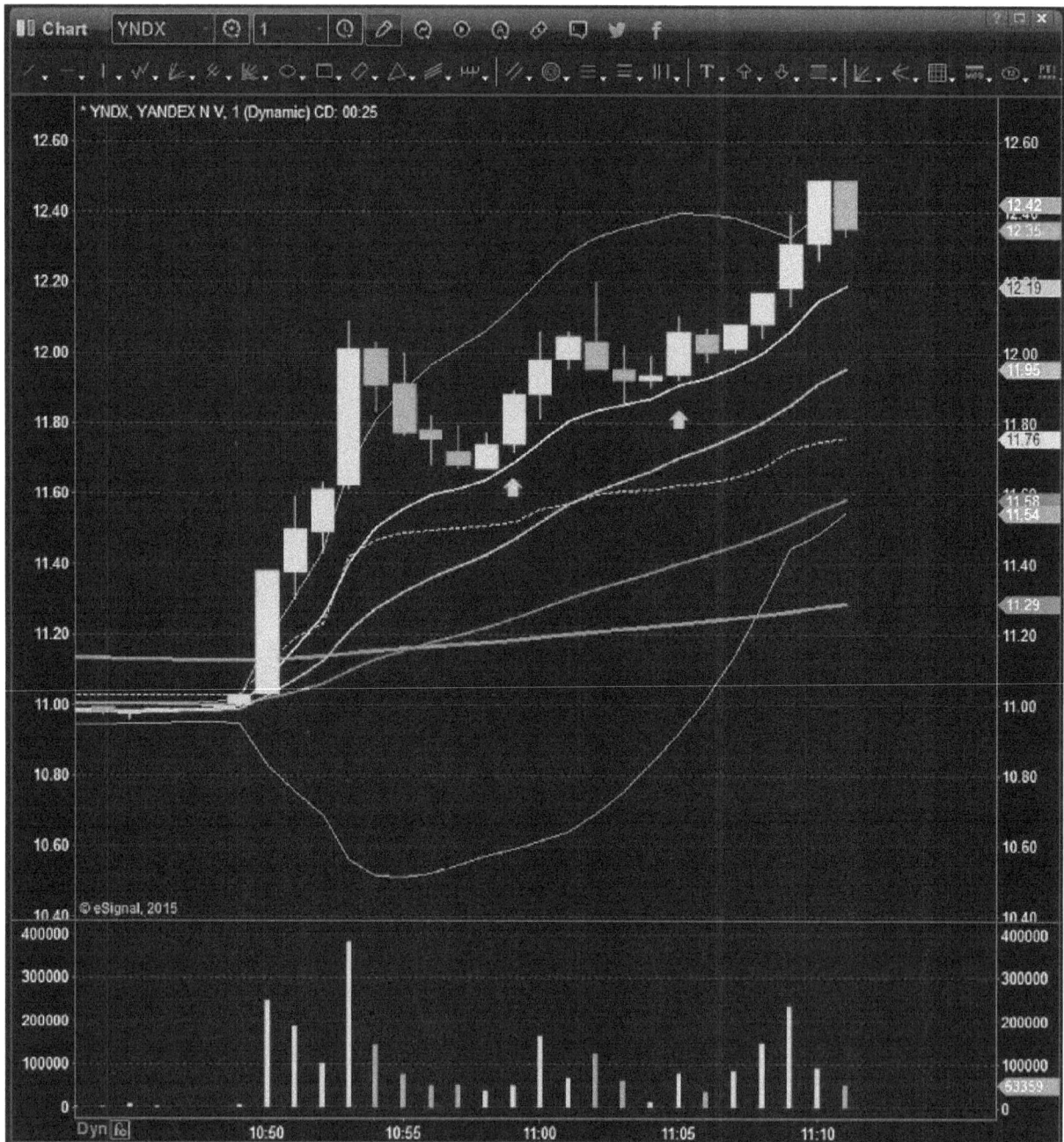

Chart of a nearly picture perfect Bull Flag. Notice the orderly pullback to the 9 EMA. This shows a clean first and second pull back opportunity. The green arrows indicate the proper entries.

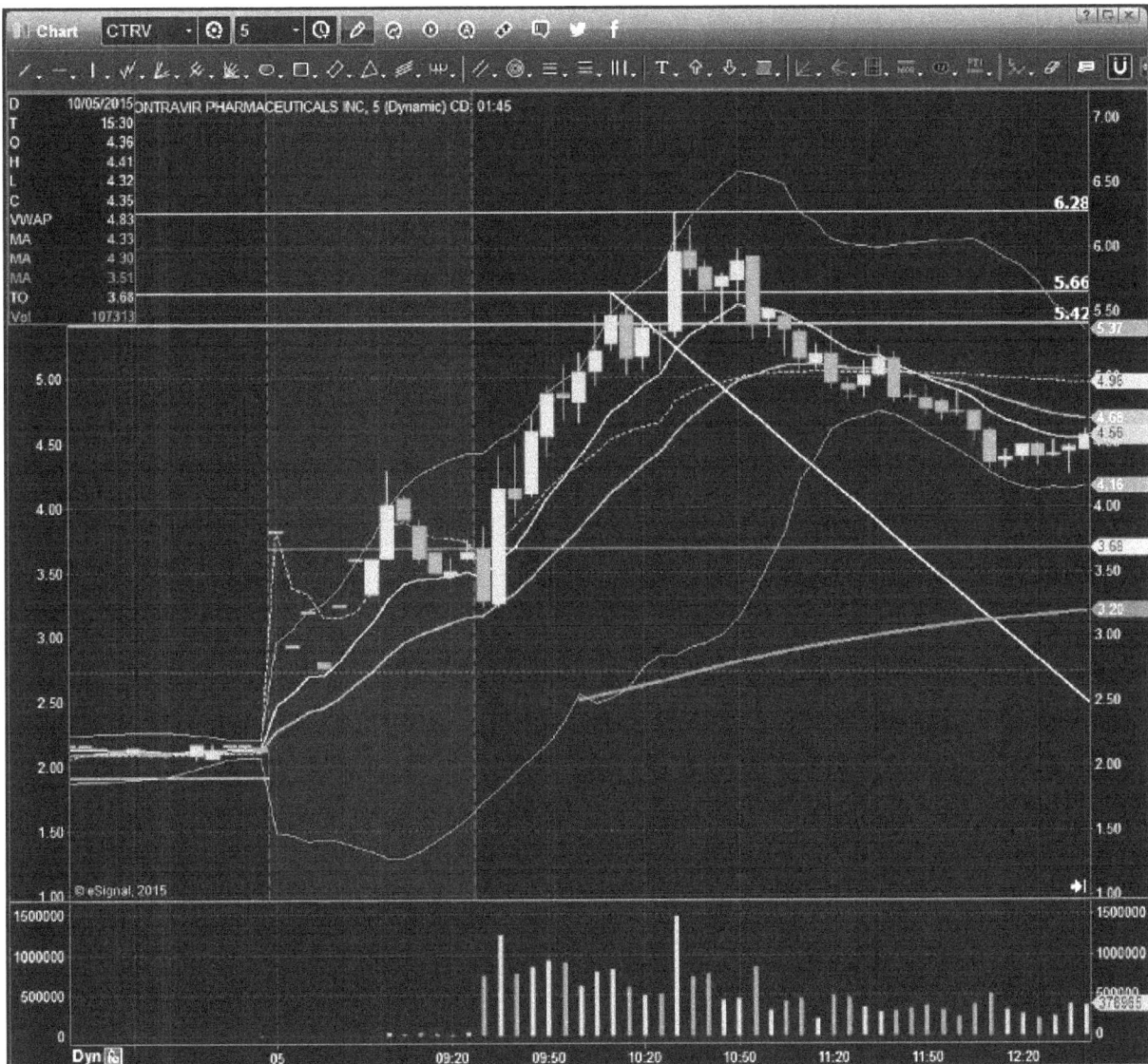

Chart of a Bull Flag. Notice the clean pullback to the 9 EMA. The entry here would have been $5.42, with a stop at the low of the pullback. Although the formation of the flag was not as clean, this bull flag breakout resulted in a volume spike as buyers rushed into the stock.

Bull Flags

Bull flags are my second favorite chart pattern. A bull flag is very similar to a flat top breakout, except with one very important difference. Unlike a flat top breakout, a bull flag will experience a slight pullback off the first strong move. I have found that bull flags produce some of my largest winning trades out of all the setups I trade. The only reason I prefer flat top breakouts is, the flat top suggests stronger bullish sentiment, because the price has not had a pull back. A typical bull flag will make a move of three to five strong, long body green candles, and then have one to three smaller red candles as it pulls back. While bull flags can be traded on any time frame, I prefer the one minute and the five minute charts. We typically look for bull flags on stocks that are already on our watch list, because we know they will trade with heavy volume due to a catalyst. I often find bull flags by watching the high of day momentum scanners. Stocks that are surging up with high relative volume, can form bull flags worth trading when they begin to pullback. This puts me into the group of traders who missed the first move, but will buy up the first and second pullbacks. The best bull flags will pullback less than 25% of the move. Unlike a flat top breakout where we buy near the high of the consolidation, during a bull flag, we purchase when the first candle makes a new high. The first candle to make a new high, versus the high of a previous candle is considered a possible turning point where momentum shifts back into the hands of the bulls. When I enter on the first candle to make a new high, I set my stop loss at the low of the pullback, and have my first profit target at the high of day price.

It is important that we do not enter bull flags at the high of day. Some new traders will mistake a bull flag for a flat top breakout and will wait to buy until the high of day price is hit. When a stock makes a quick move up, a pullback, and then a second move up, a double top is usually formed. Double tops will always be strong resistance points. Note that a flat top consists of three or more taps at the resistance price. If a stock is extremely strong it can break through the double top resistance and continue to run, but it is important to recognize the difference between a flat top breakout and a double top after a bull flag. Buying double tops usually means purchasing a stock at the high of day, and then having to sell for a loss. Sometimes a double top will turn into a flat top breakout pattern if it is given enough time to consolidate.

An important characteristic to watch for on the bull flag is strong volume during the first initial move up, low volume during the pullback, and then high volume as the stock moves back up and through the highs. If you see high volume on the pullback, it may be an indicator that the stock is actually going to reverse, instead of setting up for a second move higher. The high level of volume on the pullback suggests short sellers may be coming into the trade to push it down.

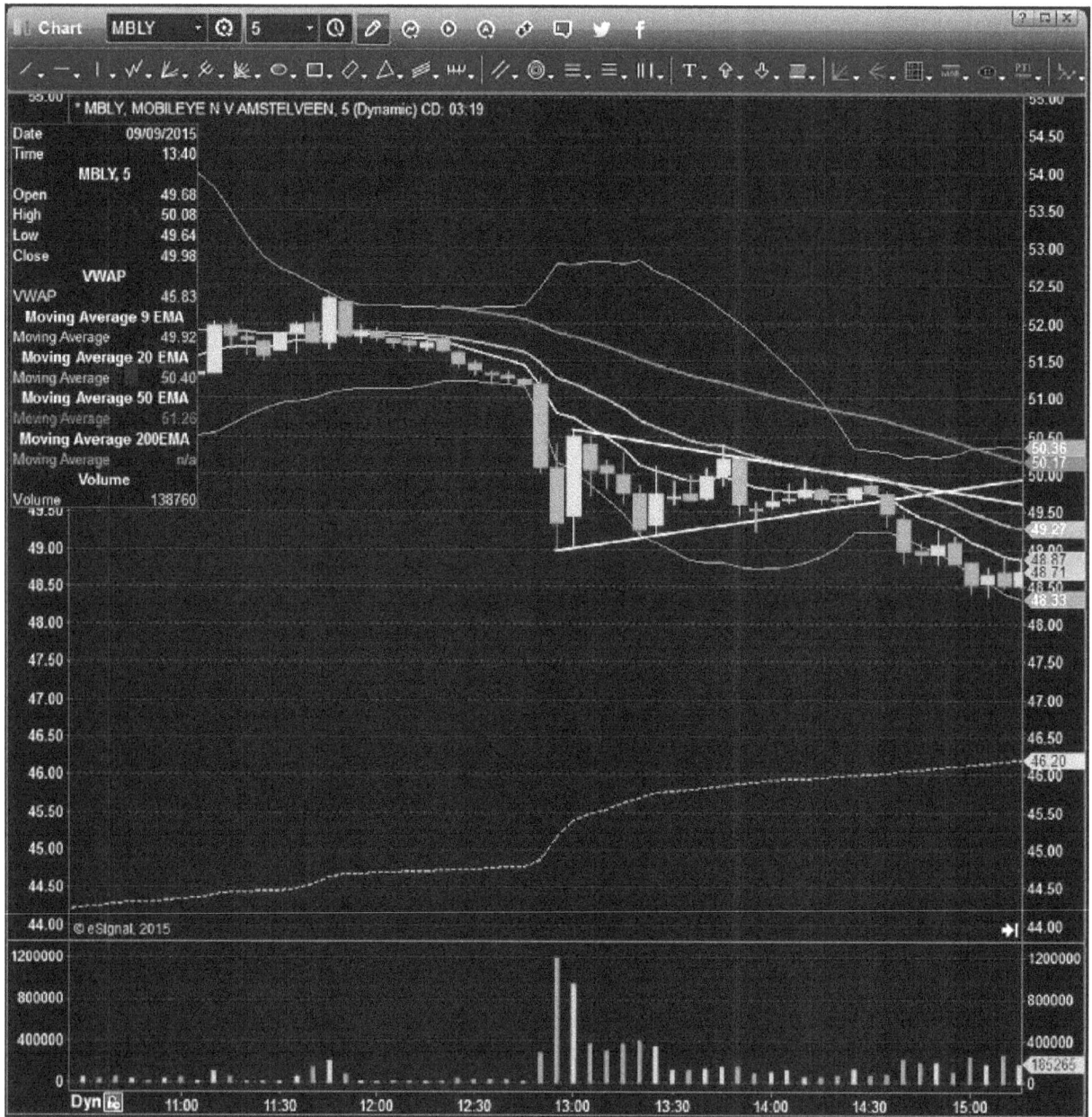

Chart of a Bear Flag. This flag was consolidating near the 9 EMA.

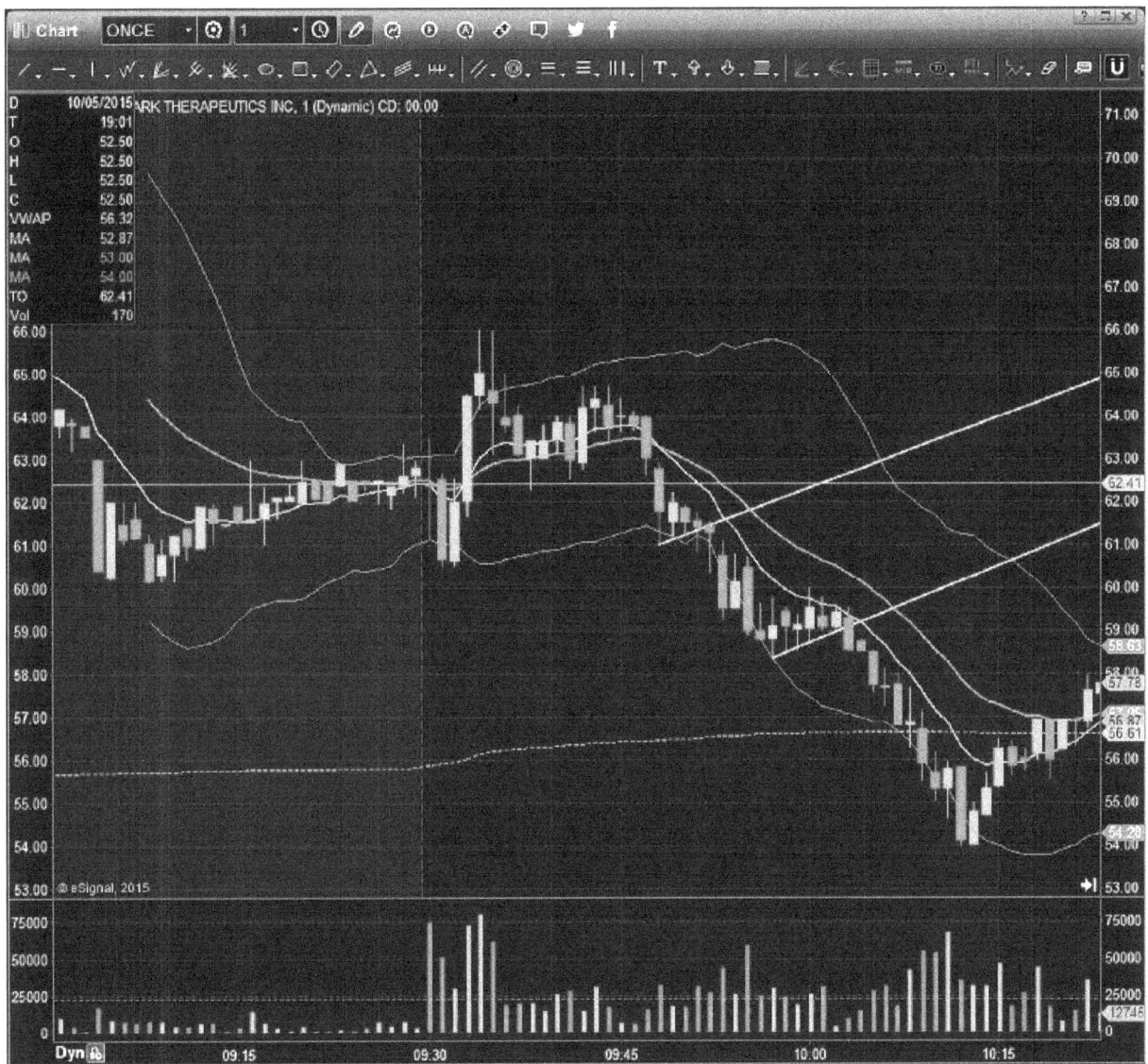

Chart of first and second Bear Flags. Both show consolidation near the 9 EMA.

Bear Flags

A bear flag is the inverse of a bull flag. We look for a strong sell off, a slight bounce on light volume, and then the first candle that makes a new low to start the next round of selling. I trade flat bottom breakdowns, but I don't usually trade bear flags unless they are extremely obvious. When I trade bear flags, they are typically flags forming on the one minute chart due to a sudden drop in prices. When news breaks and a stock quickly drops 5%, they often bounce up momentarily, before selling off again. The best bear flags are ones that occur on stocks surging with volume.

A stock that has been generally weak all day, and is forming a longer bear flag on the five minute chart, can be a good candidate for a day long fade. These are stocks that may not have news, but are simply grinding lower on volume. If a stock is forming a bear flag on lighter volume, it is important to remember that the strength or weakness of the overall market can influence the price. Since I am predominantly long biased, if I decide to short stocks, I prefer taking setups that are extremely obvious.

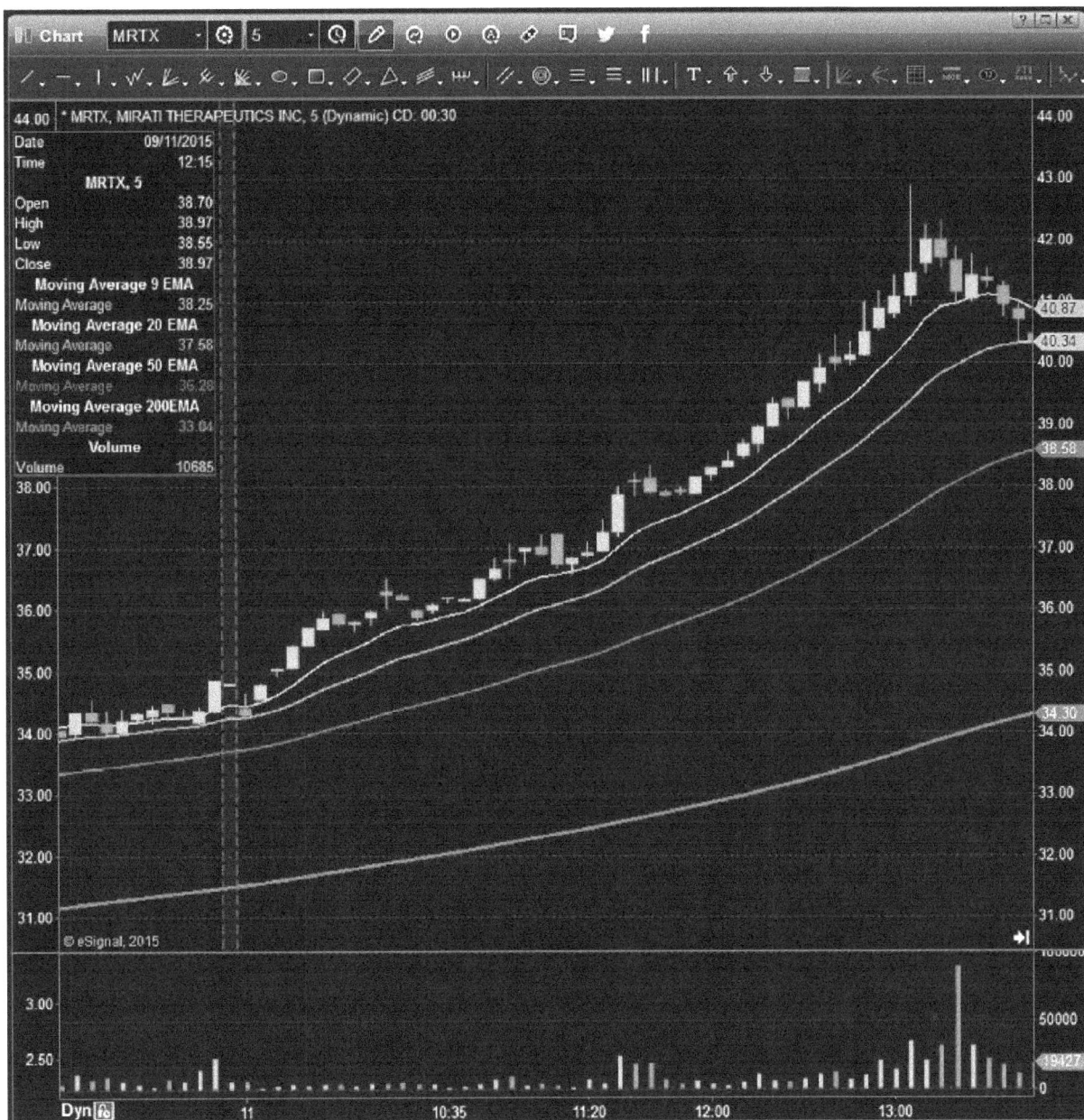

Chart of stock riding the 9 EMA all day long. Each moving average pullback represented a buying opportunity as a small flag pattern was formed.

Moving Average Retracements

At a certain point after a stock has made a quick move up, and pulls back more than three to five candles, it is no longer a bull flag. A bull flag requires a very distinctive move to the upside, and a short period of pullback before making another move up. When a stock pulls back and consolidates during the pullback, it is neither a bull flag nor a flat top breakout pattern. It is simply a flag pattern. Whenever I look at flag patterns, I like to see the stock consolidating above the support of the 9 EMA or possibly the 20 EMA. Moving average retracements will almost always be based on the five minute chart, since they are slower moving setups that require more traders to take notice. We only trade one minute setups on fast moving breakouts. The reason I like the moving average retracements is because when prices hold above the 9 EMA, it is a good indicator of strength in the trend. When a stock has pulled back beyond a typical bull flag, I usually wait for the price to actually touch the 9 EMA before taking my position. In the case where a stock has pulled back and broken the bull flag formation, we can no longer buy the first candle to make a new high. Instead we have to wait for the moving average consolidation. Many times, strong stocks will ride the 9 EMA for a period of several hours. Any pullback to the 9 EMA offers a low risk entry opportunity for these types of trending stocks.

During a 9 EMA pullback, I will buy once the price has touched the 9 EMA and set my stop at the low of the pullback or just below the moving average. I typically like to see the price has touched the 9 EMA, and is beginning to curl up slightly before taking my position. This shows me that traders are respecting the moving average as a support level. Remember, the difference between the bull flag and the 9 EMA pullback is that the 9 EMA pullback typically takes much longer to develop. When I am holding a position from a 9 EMA pullback setup, I will sell half through the high of day spike and adjust my stop to breakeven. I will hold the remaining position until I see an exit indicator.

Many conservative traders will use a strategy of only entering trades near moving average support. Entering near moving average support provides the lowest risk entry for trend based trades. Additionally, many of these traders will hold positions until a moving average is broken by the price action. In the stock chart of MRTX, you can plainly see that if you entered on the first moving average pullback after momentum picked up at 11:20am, you would have been in at about $37.00. You could have held this position until about 3:30pm, when the price broke below the 9 EMA at $41.00. This is a favorable strategy since these types of trades can provide an opportunity to participate in the market without having to take part in high speed trading. Slower moving trend based trades are generally suitable for smaller share size because the risk of exposure time is increased.

We can also trade moving average retracements to the short side for weak stocks. The rules of shorting weak stocks on the 9 EMA pop is the same as the 9 EMA pullback trade. Moving average entries provide short opportunities that I find much safer than a traditional bear flag, because they are slower moving and less volatile. The moving average support gives me confidence in the trend whether it is to the long side or the short side.

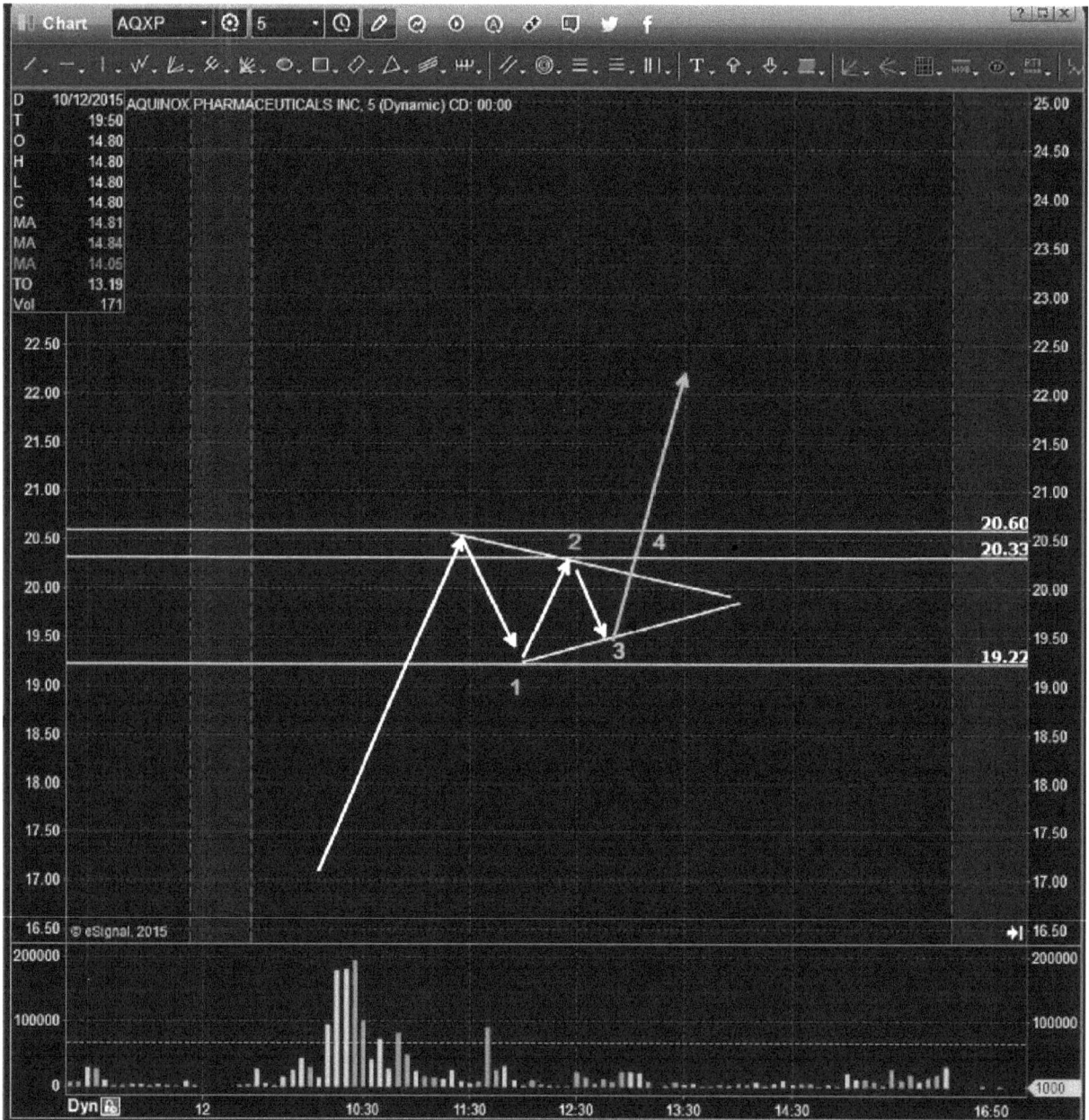

Diagram of Momentum Pullback. The entry can be seen when the high of (2) is broken. The entry is (4). Notice the (3) is a higher low versus the low of (1).

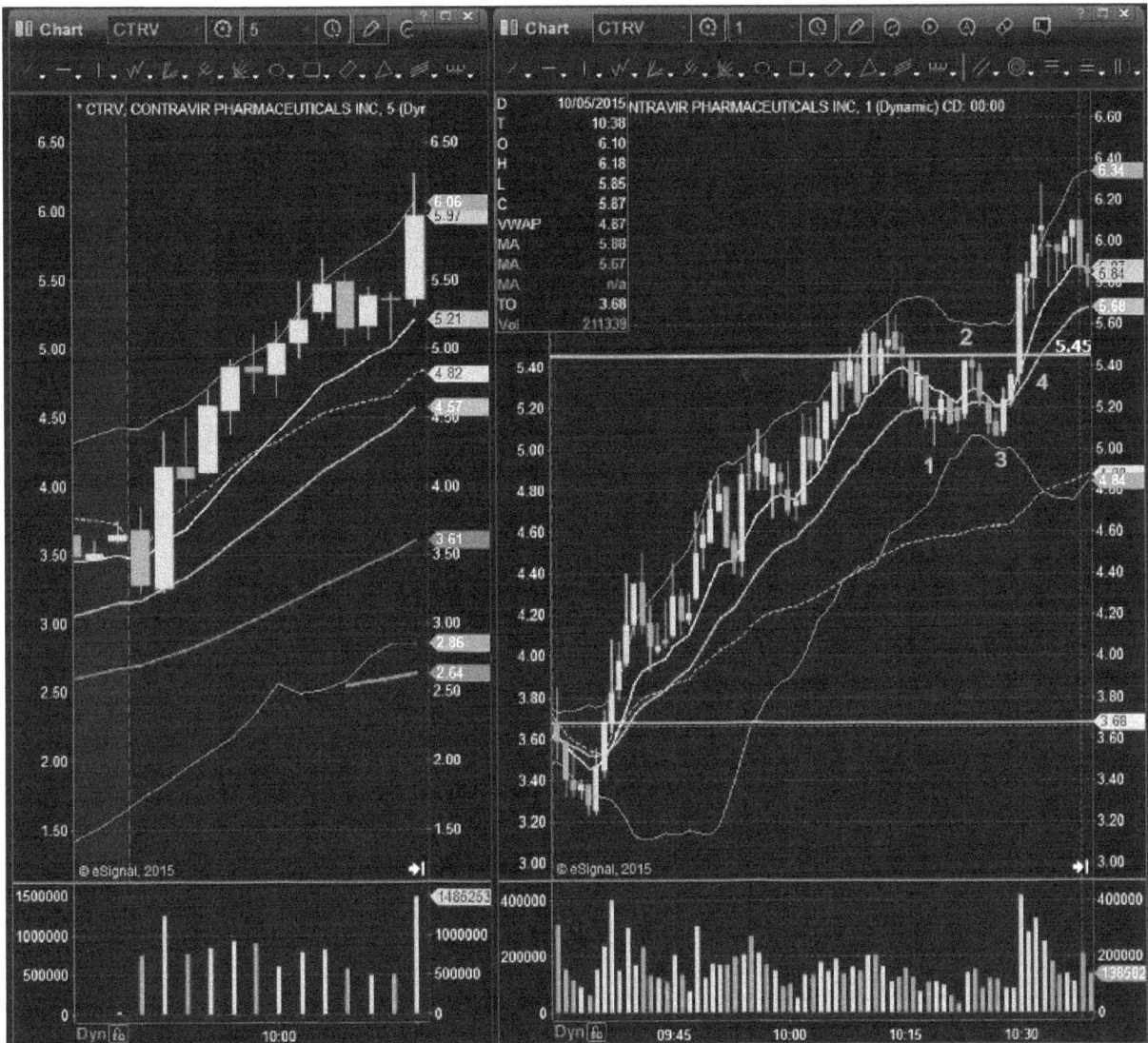

Chart showing a one minute pullback in the context of a five minute bull flag. The entry can be seen on both the five minute chart for the first candle to make a new high and on the one minute chart, when the high of (2) is broken. The entry is (4).

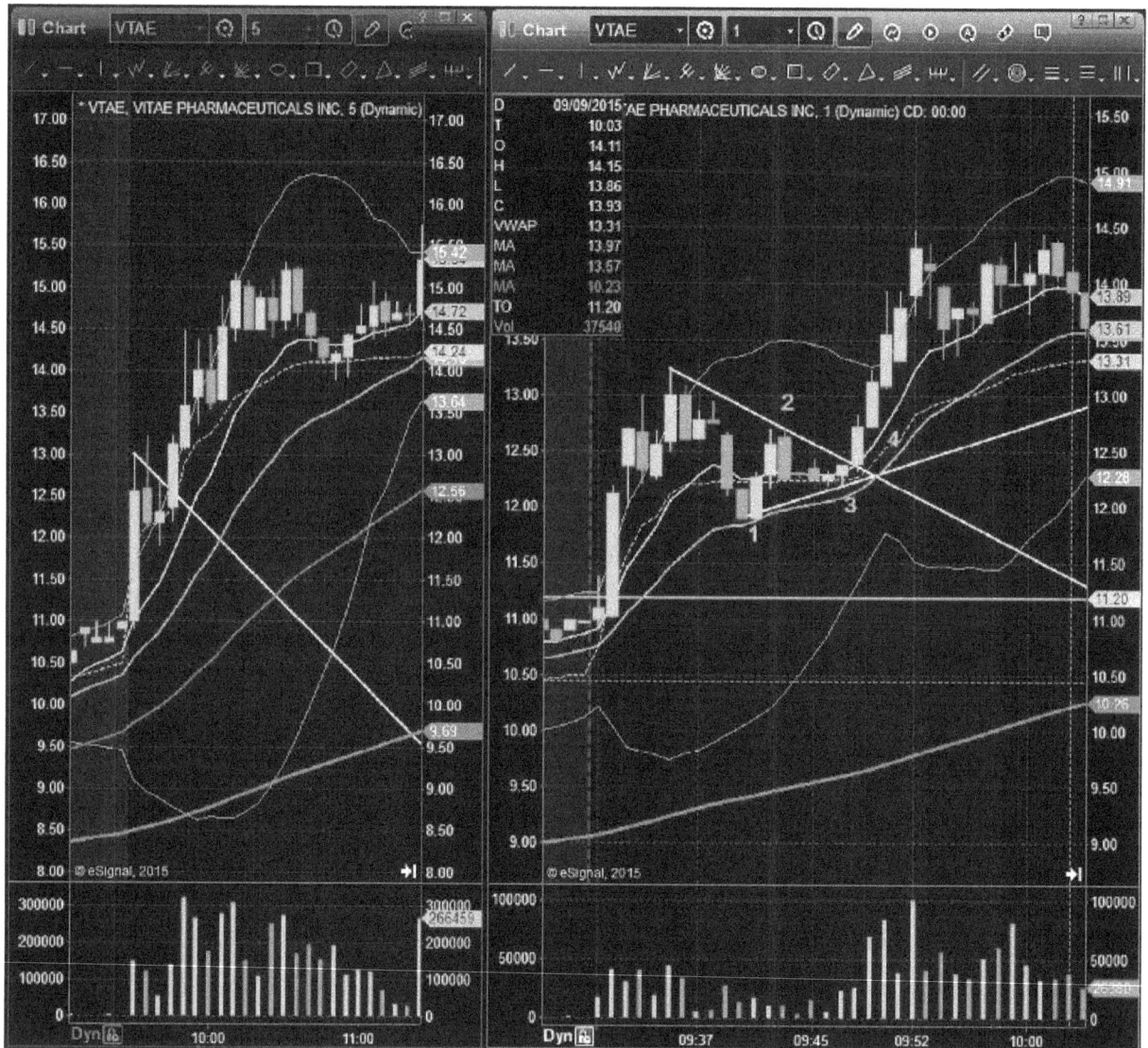

Chart showing the apex point (4) of the momentum shift. This is always the point where the price is making a new high after a short term pull back.

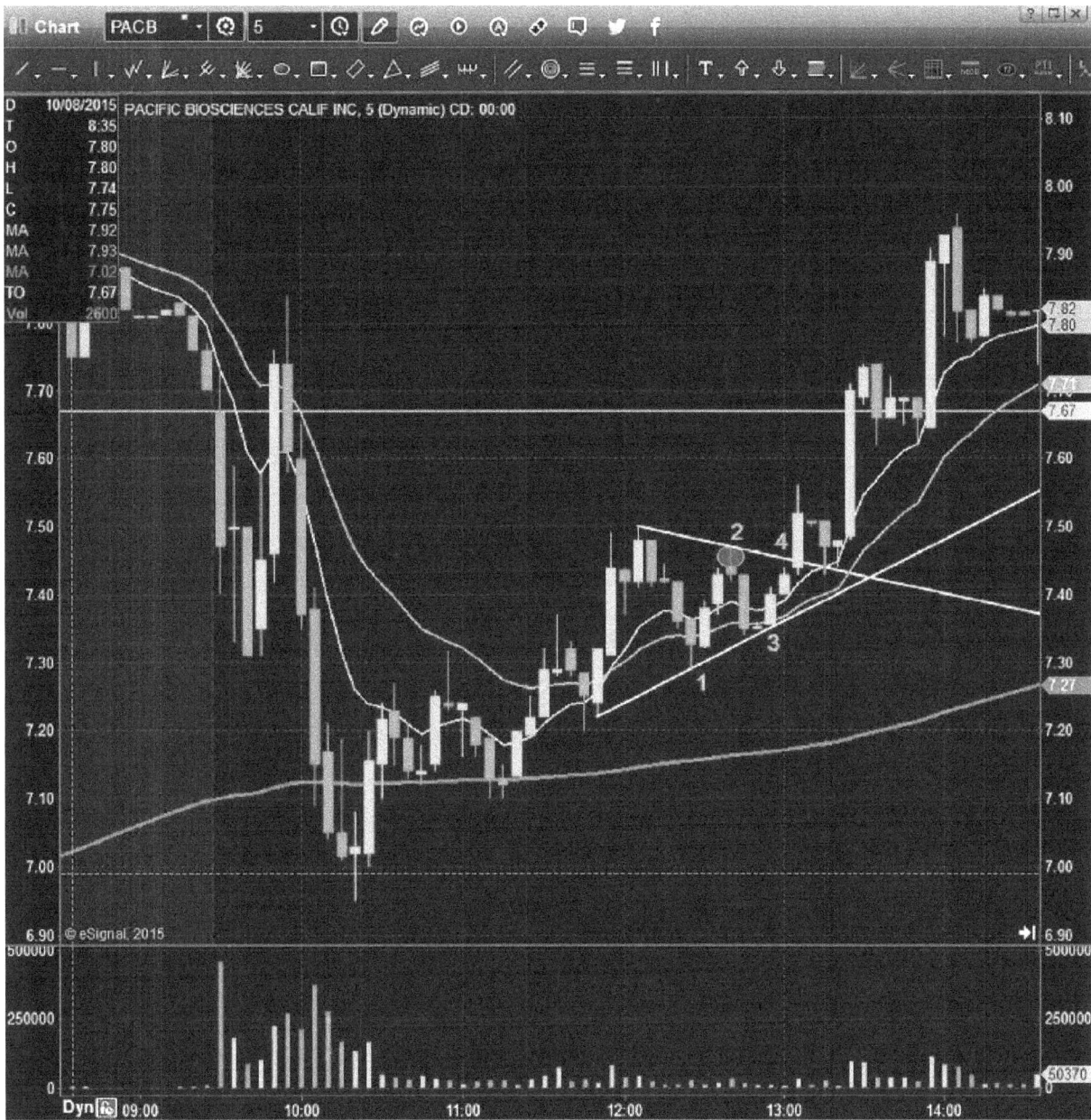

Chart showing the apex point (4) of the momentum shift.

Buying a Higher High after a Pullback during a Five Minute Uptrend

During the period of consolidation when a pullback is forming, we see different setups depending on which chart we are looking at. I always refer to the five minute chart when looking for setups. When we have a stock that has given us a long bias on the daily chart, and we have a strong trend on the five minute chart, we will look for a pullback entry. In the case of the above example on CTRV, you can see that the price pulled back on the one minute chart below the one minute moving averages. The stock pulls back to price (1), then pivots and pops up to price (2), then pivots again and pulled back to price (3). It is important to note that the pullback of (3) was a higher price than (1). This is important because the price could have continued lower than the pivot of price (1), and continued a short term retracement. During this time we can see on the five minute chart that the price was touching the 9 EMA. The pivot at price (2), is the place we need to see break in order to enter this position. A break of price (2), on the one minute chart will indicate the trend is being restored as the price is making a higher high. What makes this pattern on the one minute especially strong is the fact that the break of price (2), will also be the first five minute candle to make a new high. I always watch both the one minute and the five minute charts, and look for them to give me entry signals around the same price. That price will be the apex point where a pattern either breaks out or breaks down.

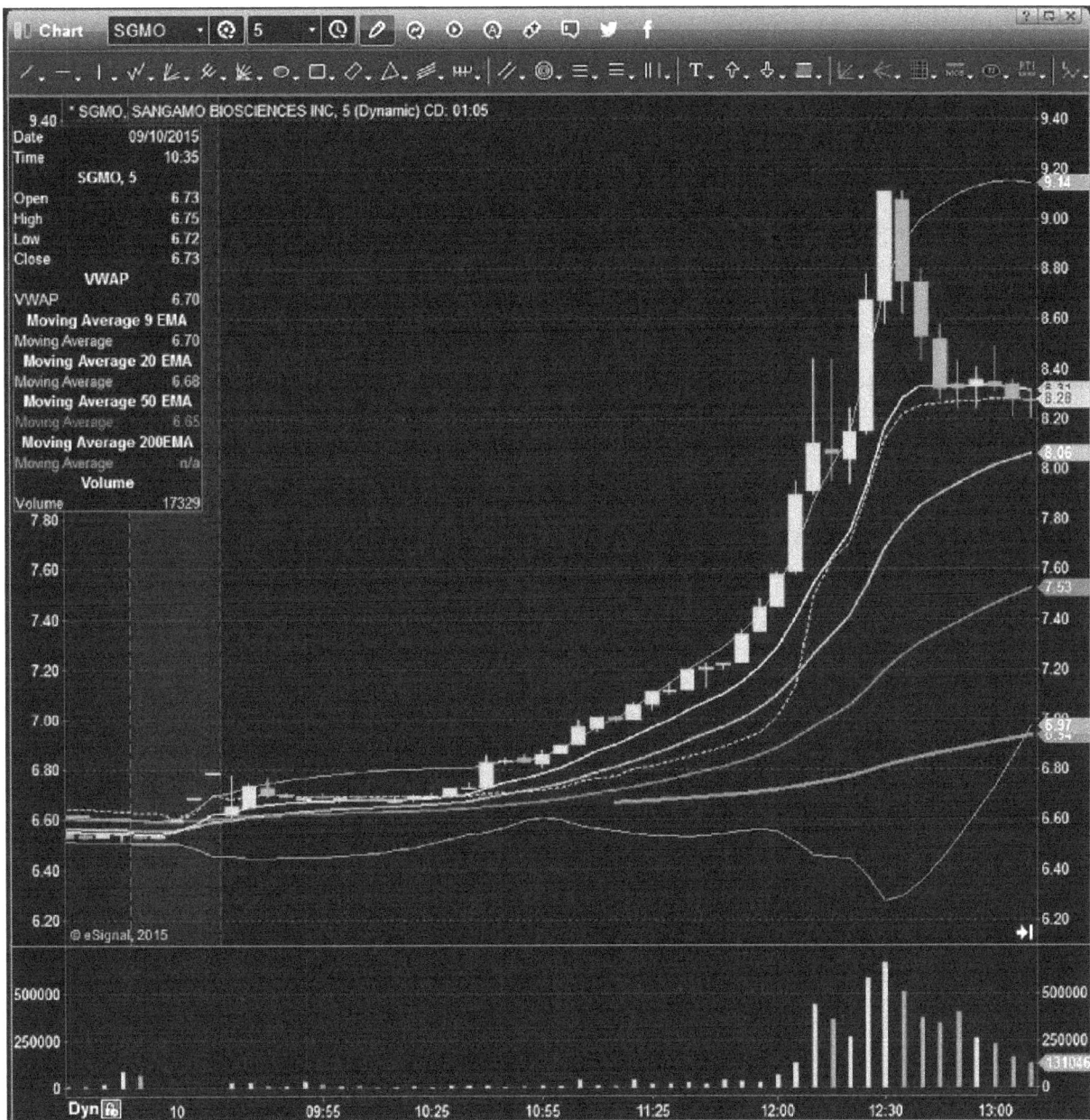

Chart of Parabolic Mover. Note the retracement to the moving average at 3pm. This retracement would be the profit target for short sellers who shorted the stock during the squeeze.

Chart of a Parabolic Mover. In this example the 9 EMA did not appear to provide support.

Parabolic Moves

As day traders, we love when stocks make parabolic moves. A

parabolic move is when a stock basically goes straight up or straight down. This pattern is almost always the result of a strong catalyst and a strong daily chart. Parabolic movers are stocks that will be irrationally strong or weak. We have seen stocks lose half their value in one day while others surge up over 1000%. These types of extreme moves are not uncommon in the markets today.

There are a few ways to trade parabolic movers. If I want to participate in the momentum, I will enter parabolic stocks on a momentary pullback in the form of a bull flag or a flat top breakout. Typically these patterns will be on the one minute chart since the stock is moving very quickly. If I can get an entry, I will ride the momentum as long as possible, but I will make sure I sell half of my position quickly and adjust my stop to breakeven. It is not uncommon to quickly be up and then have the price drop right back to breakeven or to a loss. Buying a parabolic mover almost always means chasing, and chasing can be risky. We have to mitigate the risk involved with trading these types of stocks by using smaller positions, until we have built up a profit cushion on the name and can afford to take a larger risk.

The second way to trade parabolic stocks is to wait for the reversal. We cannot always time the entry or predict when a stock is going to run 100%, but we know almost all big moves will get reversed at some point. The challenge is that some stocks will look like they are about to reverse when they are up 100%, but end up running to 200% instead. Trying to guess the top or bottom of a parabolic move can be just as risky as chasing the momentum. As we have already said, day trading is risky, but we can mitigate risk by avoiding the most dangerous setups. Parabolic movers are the highest risk setups we will discuss. They provide high risk, but high reward opportunities. I generally reduce my share size when trading these types of stocks as a risk management technique. If I am going to try to take a reversal trade, I will always begin with a quarter of my planned position size. This allows the stock to continue to squeeze up without stopping me out.

We may have the right idea, but the wrong timing. The advantage of scaling in is that we do not have to pick the exact reversal point. We can add a quarter size, add another quarter, and then add full size once the reversal confirms. Another advantage to scaling in is that once a reversal has been confirmed, we will often be really far away from the stop because of the range of parabolic stocks. Whether you trade parabolic stocks with momentum setups, reversal setups or both, remember that when stocks start to surge up, it is easy to think about all the profit potential and forget about risk management. I always try to stay focused on my risk levels and use smaller positions to reduce the emotions and greed that are involved with big movers.

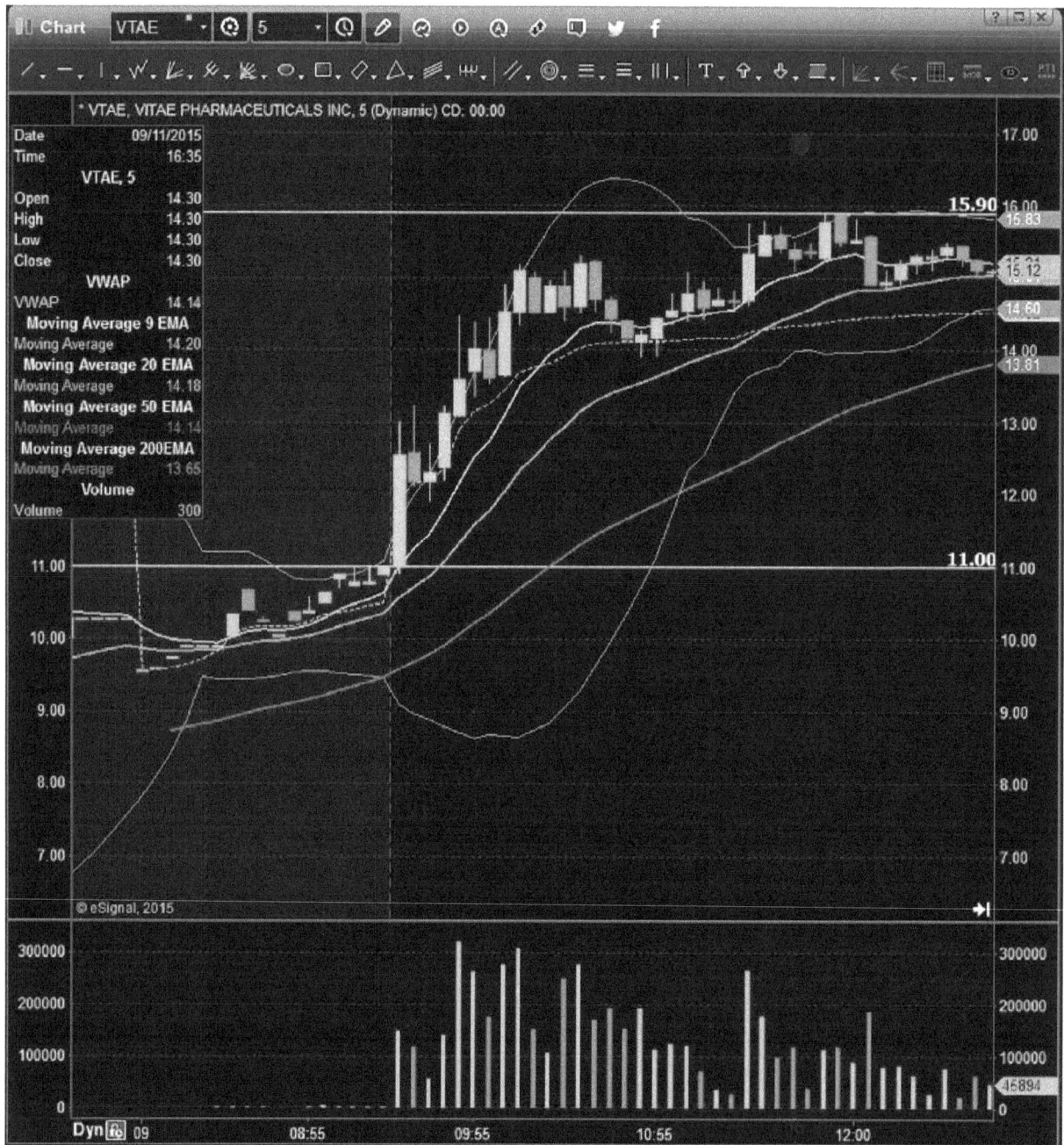

Chart of stock gapping up and squeezing 40% at the market open.

Gap and Go Momentum Strategy

I developed the Gap and Go strategy after realizing a pattern with stocks that are strong in the pre-market session, surging when the market opens at 9:30 AM. The first advantage of trading these gappers as soon as the bell rings, is that the stocks that are strong in the pre-market session will almost always trade on high relative volume during the day. Many day traders do not take trades for the first five minutes of the market because of the extreme level of volatility. I realized I can capitalize on this volatility by using the pre-market charts as a gauge of the strength in individual stocks. It is important to note that the Gap and Go strategy works best on stocks under $20. Gap and Go stocks priced above $20, typically require smaller size to accommodate larger price ranges in the first few minutes of trading.

To find Gap and Go candidates, I look at my stock scanning window for the biggest percentage gappers. This shows all the stocks gapping up at least 4% versus the previous days close. Sometimes a stock will be gapping up, but will only have 100 shares of volume in the pre-market session. I usually disregard these stocks because they lack volume to confirm the move. When I find a stock that is gapping up more than 4%, and has more than 50k shares of pre-market volume, I consider it a gap and go contender. The price must be consolidating near the top of its pre-market range and there must be a catalyst driving the move. If a stock gapped up 30% and pulled back, and is now gapping up only 10%, I usually do not trade it because it has already shown weakness during pre-market trading. If I am unsure of the news, I will look through press releases to see if the company just reported earnings, issued a press release of some type, if there is a price target upgrade, or in the case of biotech and pharmaceutical stocks, I will check for FDA approvals or results from clinical trials. This information is readily available online but can also be accessed by asking fellow traders. If I cannot find any catalyst to account for the move, I will typically be very cautious about taking a trade right out of the gates on that stock.

The Gap and Go strategy requires a combination of fundamental and technical analysis. As day traders, we are primarily technical traders, but when a stock is surging up pre-market we need to understand why. I do not dig into reading the entire earnings report or press releases, but I recognize the importance of good quality news versus subpar news. Remember, that unconfirmed news sources should always be considered suspect.

Once I have done my due diligence and researched the catalyst, I will begin to map out the triggers and windows on the daily chart. It is important to remember that a stock with a strong catalyst can override all daily support or resistance areas. The most important levels for me to determine are my entry price and my stop price. The best Gap and Go candidates will already show a flat top breakout or a bull flag pattern in the pre-market chart. It is also worth noting that I do not usually trade pre-market unless a stock has more than 500k in pre-market volume. I prefer to wait for the market to open because that is when the big volume comes in.

Each morning, I create a watch list of two to four stocks that are good Gap and Go candidates. As I have said before, I want to trade the most obvious setups, and that is the same with the Gap and Go trades. I want to be trading the biggest percentage gapper with the most volume, because it is the stock everyone will be watching. More traders watching it means more volume at the breakout spots. Once I have mapped out the levels on the daily chart and marked the pre-market highs and lows, I am ready to prepare orders for when the market opens at 9:30 AM.

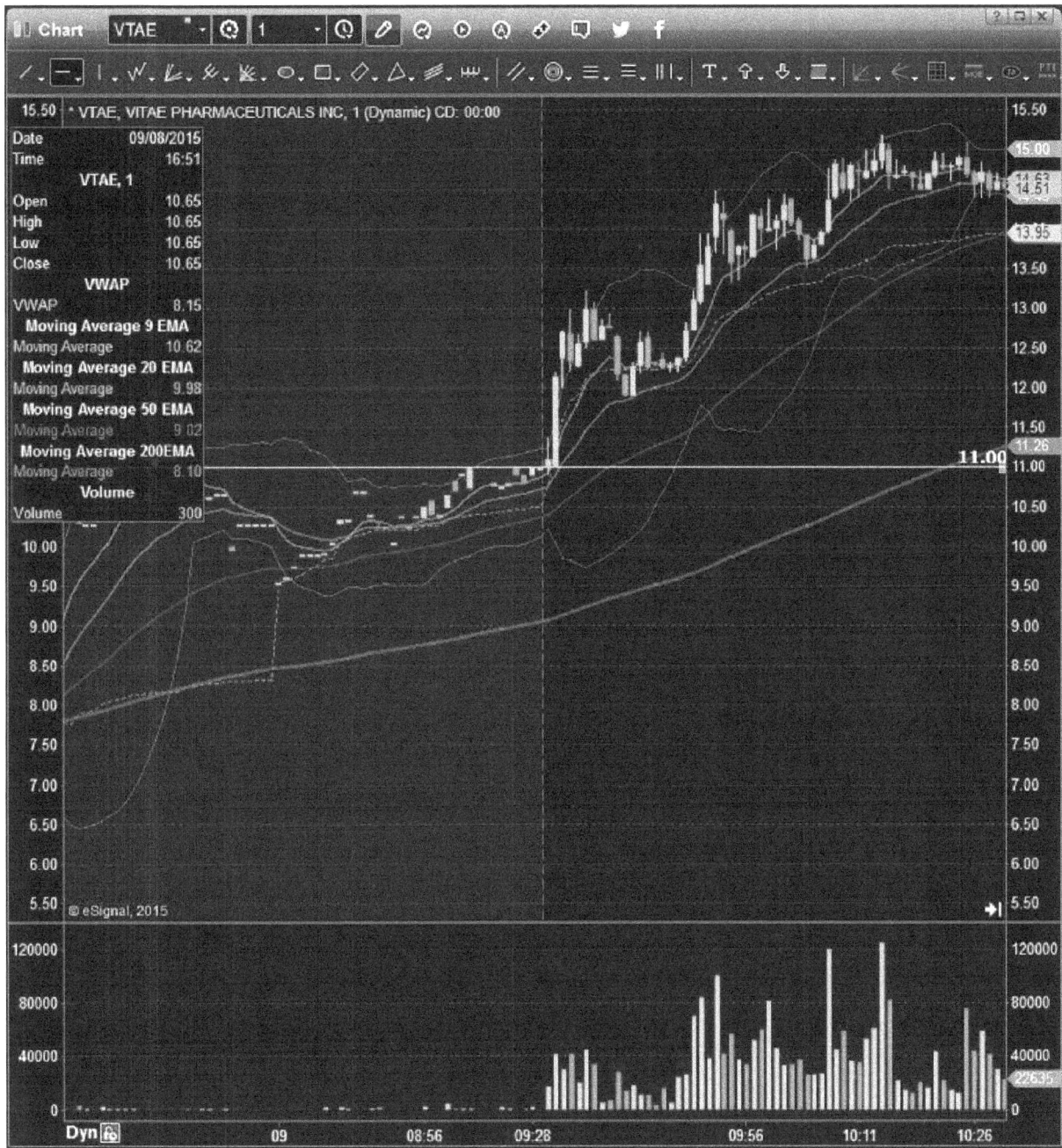

Chart with entry setup at $11.00 for a Flat Top Breakout and a break of Pre-Market Highs. This Gap and Go trade resulted in a near 20% profit in the first five minutes of trading.

Gap and Go - Buying the Bull Flag or Flat Top Breakout

If the pre-market chart already has a clear bull flag or flat top breakout pattern, I will simply trade the flag pattern. In the case of the bull flag, I will buy the first one minute or five minute candle to make a new high, and set my stop at the low of the pullback. I will hold this position until I have reached a profit target or exit indicator. My absolute favorite entry on Gap and Go stocks is buying the pre-market high, when we have a well-defined flat top breakout pattern holding above moving average support. Since the flat top will coincide with pre-market highs, if it also lines up just below a whole dollar, it is a very powerful setup. Additionally, if we can see a heavy offer on the Level2 when the market opens, it confirms the resistance at the apex point of the pattern. In order to break the apex point, a lot of buyers need to step in and buy up the shares sitting on the Ask. When it looks like the shares are almost all gone, I will place my order to try to jump in just seconds before the break. If I jump in too soon, there is the risk that not all the shares will get bought up and the resistance will hold. If I jump in too late, I will miss the breakout and my opportunity to trade a winner. Timing is very important on Gap and Go trades. This requires the use of the best trading tools, including direct access routing and hot keys. Once that apex point breaks, Gap and Go stocks will often make a quick and sometimes dramatic break through the resistance level. I will typically look to take profit on that first surge, and then quickly adjust my stop to breakeven to protect the winner. We will review the exit indicators later in this chapter. In one of our best Gap and Go stocks, we took a position at $2.50 and sold on the move up to $5.00, for a 100% move in less than 15 minutes of trading. Anyone waiting for the market to open and who had just begun looking for trades, would have missed that opportunity.

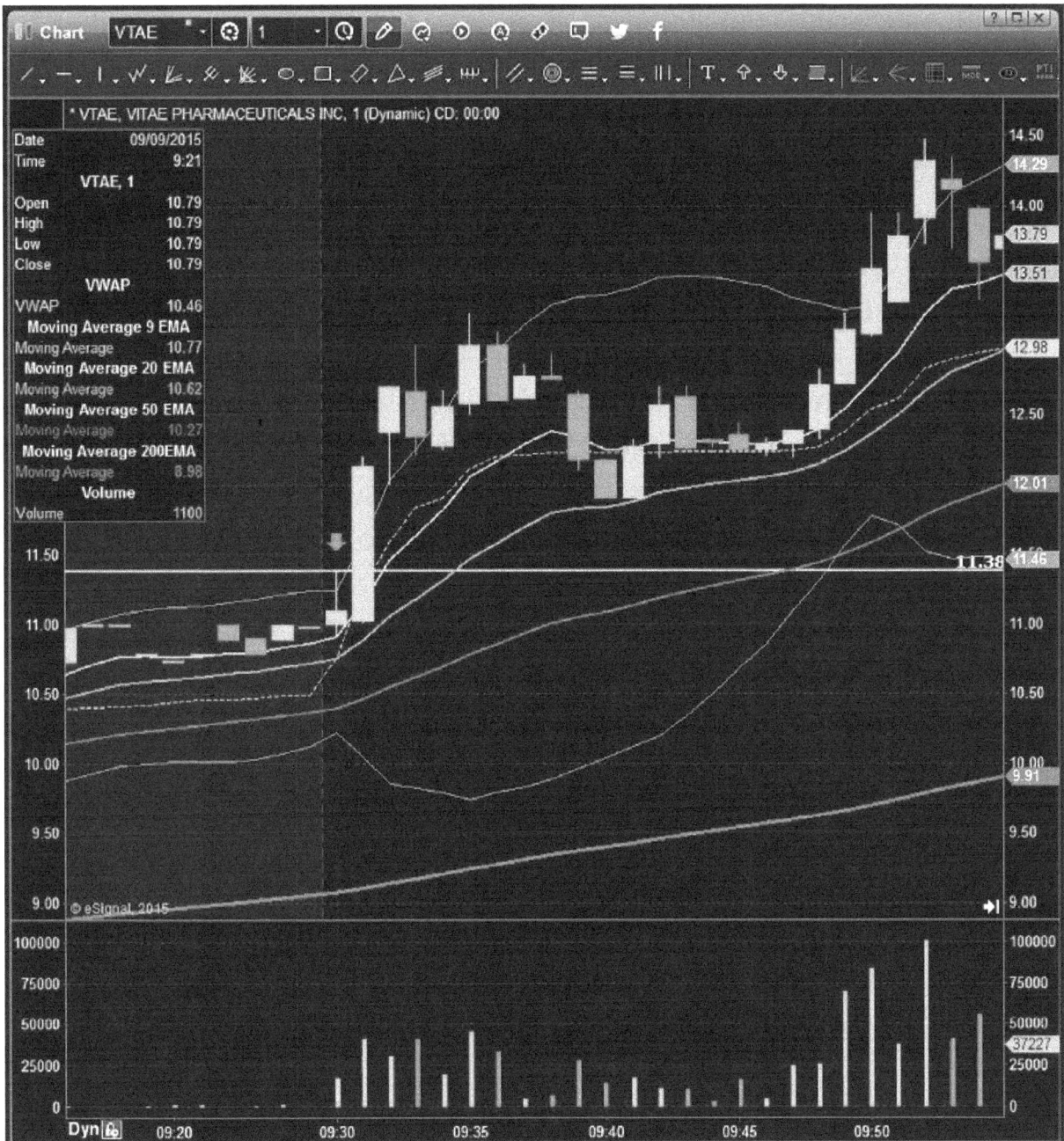

Chart of buying a one minute open range breakout $11.38.

Gap and Go - Buying the One Minute Opening Range Breakout (ORB)

When a Gap and Go candidate opens in between support and resistance levels, I use the first one minute candle as my trigger candle. The top of the first one minute candle is my entry price, and the low is my stop. If I enter a one minute ORB trade, and it immediately drops back down and breaks the low of the first one minute candle, I will stop out. I will only buy if the second one minute candle breaks the high of the first one minute candle. This is called a one minute opening range breakout (ORB). Occasionally, the resistance at the top of the first one minute candle will be noticeable on the Level2, but not always. Some traders use this exact same opening range breakout strategy with five minute candles or 15 minute candles. On stocks gapping up, I use the one minute chart instead of the five minute chart in order to react quickly to the volatility. If the one minute ORB has not occurred in the first couple of minutes, I may switch to the five minute chart and wait for a five minute ORB. If we do not get an ORB in the first fifteen or twenty minutes, I move on to a different stock on my watch list. In the event of a profitable one minute ORB trade, we may look to take additional trades on the first pullback. A good Gap and Go stock will provide multiple opportunities.

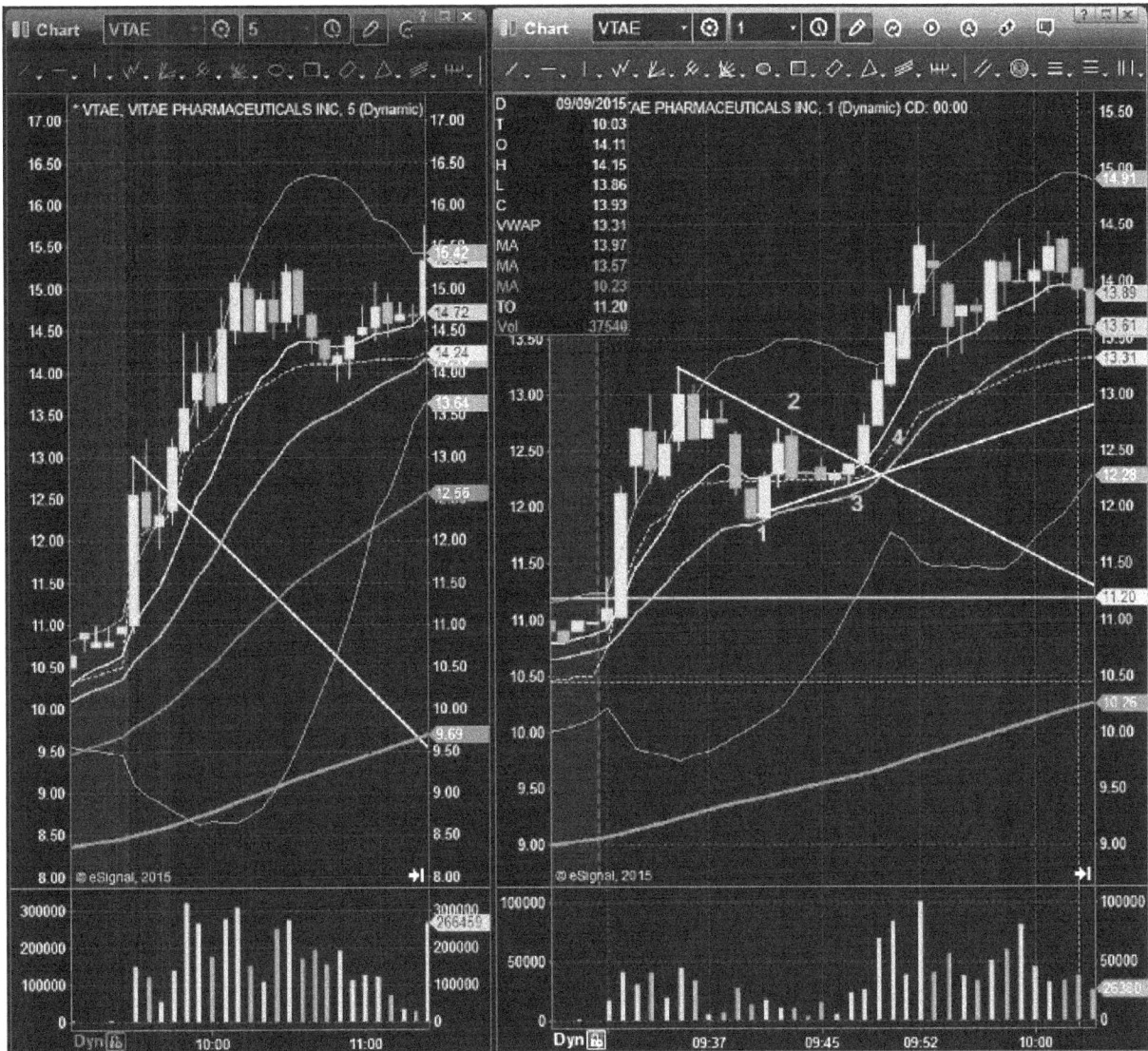

Chart of Buying the 1st pullback. The price after the red arrow broke the high of the previous one minute high, restoring the momentum and the trend. On the five minute chart, this was forming a bull flag.

Gap and Go - Buying the first pullback

Sometimes there will be a great Gap and Go trade, and you will miss the first entry on the pre-market flag breakout or the one minute ORB. In these cases, or in the case where I simply did not have that gapper on close watch, I look to get in on the first pullback. The first pullback must take the form of either a traditional bull flag, flat top breakout or

9 EMA pullback. Buying the first pullback is probably the most conservative way to trade Gap and Go stocks, because it does not require you to take a trade in the first two to three minutes of the market open. I can be very profitable trading at the open, but for beginner traders, it can be too volatile and too risky. Beginner traders may find it easier to trade the first pullback on gapping stocks. The best Gap and Go stocks will break out of the first and second pullbacks.

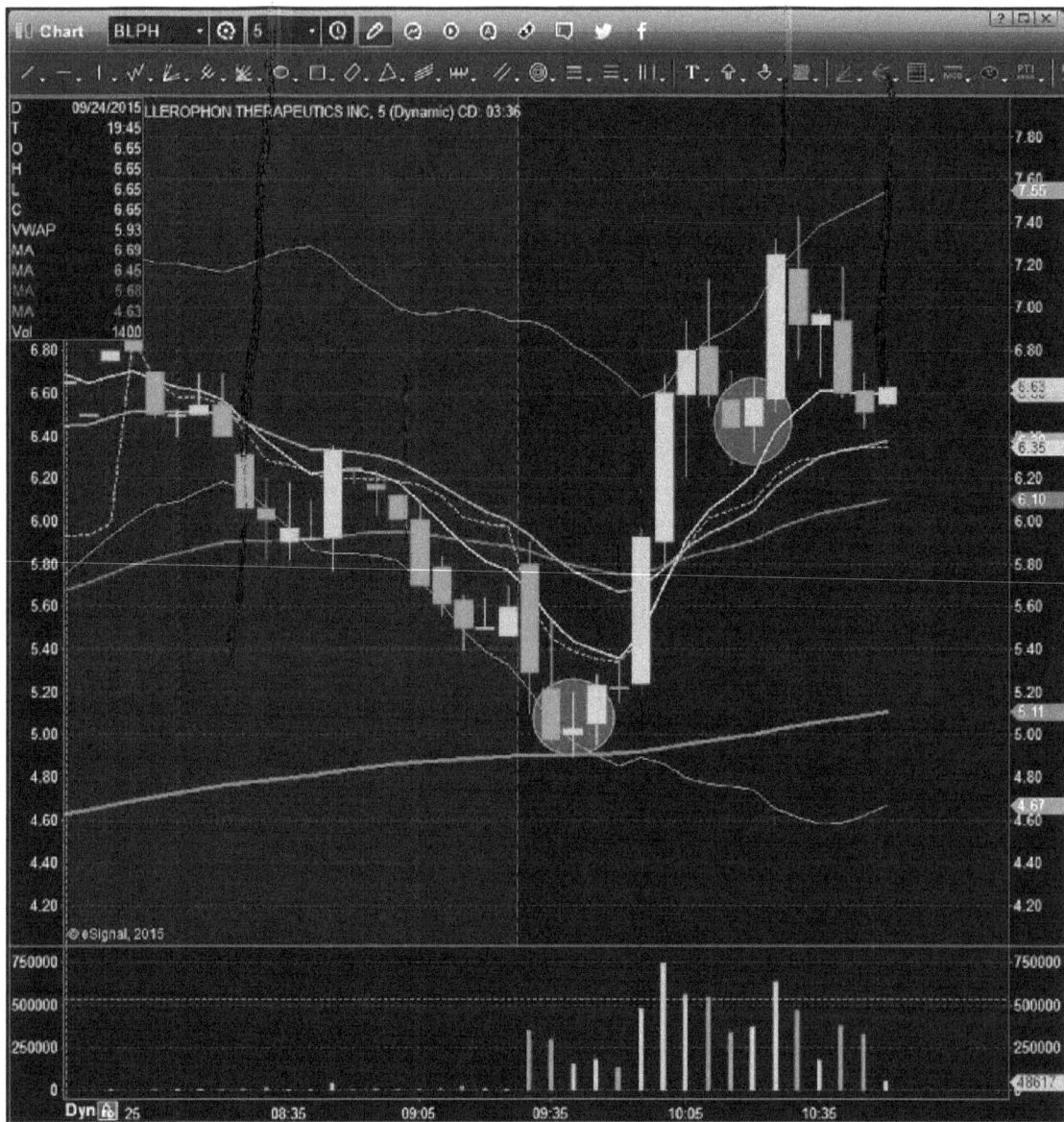

Chart of Red to Green Move. Price went red on the day versus the

open price, then surged back up. The first entry was the first five minute candle to make a new high. This stock was so strong it setup for a second entry on a bull flag pattern.

Gap and Go - Red to Green

There are times when a beautiful Gap and Go candidate opens and sells off hard right out of the gates. These stocks may be unable to break the top of the pre-market flag or may open in between support and resistance and experience a quick sell off at the open. Regardless of the reason, the only potential setup left for these Gap and Go stocks is the Red to Green move. A Red to Green move is when the price of the stock drops below the open price and then surges back through the open price. This has the effect of making the stock go from red on the day to green on the day, versus the open price. Despite the early sign of weakness, Red to Green moves can be powerful, because anyone that decided to short the stock on weakness at the open will most likely cover as it breaks through the open price. The added buying volume of shorts covering and long biased traders getting in, can create an explosive breakout. The biggest risk with this setup is that the stock has already shown a tendency for weakness and it could be quickly overpowered by sellers again. I enter a Red to Green move on the first candle to make a new high after the washout. This trade can be taken on either the one minute or the five minute chart. Once I am in the trade, I will immediately set a mental stop at the low of day, and look to sell half my position as soon as I have made what I was risking. Once I have sold half, I will adjust my stop to breakeven and hold the position as long as possible. On strong Red to Green moves, we will have opportunities to trade the first pullback after the breakout, and possibly the break of pre-market highs. If I buy a Red to Green setup, and it immediately goes back to red on the day, I will sell for a loss. I consider that an immediate exit indicator and in general, weakness in the stock.

Momentum and Gap and Go Entry Requirements

All Gap and Go setups should meet the following entry requirements:

1. 100k in volume in the first one minute of trading when the market opens (Gap and Go trades)

2. 1mil in volume (Momentum Trading Strategy trades)

3. We can reasonably achieve 2:1 profit loss ratio

4. The stock should have high relative volume of at least 2

5. The pattern must be obvious and clear. We know even the best patterns do not always work

6. Ideally, the entry point will be close the 9 EMA or 20 EMA support level

7. Ideally, the float is under 50 million shares, with under 10 million having the most potential. The exception is that VWAP trading strategies can be used on heavier float stocks

8. Ideally, the stock will have a good catalyst

9. Ideally, the stock will have a clean daily chart with windows and triggers

Entering a Momentum Trade

When I am preparing to enter a momentum trade, I pull up the Level2 and first look at the spreads and the amount of volume. I typically want to see tight spreads of five cents or less. A stock with wide spreads will be more difficult to manage because they can quickly pop or drop without giving us time to get out.

One Minute Entries

Many of my Momentum Trading Strategies require buying based on one minute chart patterns. In order to take a one minute setup, we need extremely high relative volume. We need so much volume that the five minute candles are too big to use for risk management. When I enter a trade, I always have an exact price in mind that I want to buy at. The price is usually the apex of the pattern, in the case of a one minute Gap and Go ORB, it is the top of the one minute candle. In the case of a Flat Top Breakout, it is the price of the flat top. I prepare my limit order in my brokerage account, with an offset a few cents above the price, and then watch the Level2. By using a slight offset, I can usually get filled. If I see a heavy amount of resistance at the price where I want to enter, I will wait until that seller begins to move or the shares get bought up before hitting the buy button. Just before it looks like the price is going to break, I jump in. Since I am buying at the apex point with most of my momentum trades, I expect almost immediate resolution. If i do not see immediate resolution, that by itself is an indicator of weakness, and a cue to possibly reduce my position size or exit completely. Using the one minute chart, I always start with a half sized position. I never like to start with full size when I am buying at the apex point, because if I am wrong, I will experience a big loss. Additionally, whenever I first enter a trade, I am exposed to my max risk level. Instead, I start with half size and double up if I can adjust my stop to breakeven. If I cannot double up, I will happily take the win with the smaller position size knowing I managed my risk properly.

Five Minute Entries

Since I have more confidence in five minute patterns I will typically take larger size on my first order. With five minute chart patterns, I am still buying the apex of the pattern, the breaking point of the bull flag or the top of the flat top breakout. In the case of Gap and Go trades, the only setups I might use on the five minute chart would be the five minute ORB, the first pullback, or a Red to Green move. The majority of my Gap and Go trades start on the one minute chart with the first entry. Midday momentum trades of strong stocks will typically form patterns on the five minute chart. Midday is a risky time to trade off the one minute chart because the volume is typically a lot lighter than the first hour of trading. Unless there is breaking news or extremely heavy volume, I typically use the five minute chart for momentum trades past 10 AM. When I jump in, I immediately set my stop at the low of the pullback, just below the 9 EMA, or just below the ascending support line, depending on the setup.

Profit Targets

Momentum trades can be extremely quick. I have been in stocks that surged up 50% in a matter of minutes and then came all the way back down and ended the day red. This means whenever I am up the amount I was risking on the trade, I will sell half my position. On momentum trades that have the ideal set of entry requirements, with a good daily chart and a strong catalyst, I may hold the position a little bit longer before scaling out. Alternatively, if I enter a momentum trade on a one minute setup with the intention of doubling on the five minute confirmation, or on the high of day break such as on a bull flag, I will adjust my stop to breakeven. When I double up, I am no longer at risk of losing money on the trade. Anytime I can get in a trade with a breakeven stop, I am in the drivers seat. I have a free opportunity for a big winner.

Estimating profit targets on momentum trades can be difficult. With reversal trades, we look for a bounce back up to the 9 EMA or the VWAP, but with momentum trades, we have to look to the the daily chart or look for technical areas of resistance. We typically find resistance around half dollars and whole dollars ($10.00, $10.50, $11.00, etc). I try to take profit if I am in a momentum trade and it is approaching a logical resistance point. I then adjust my stop to breakeven or adjust my stop into the profit zone. I always want to keep a partial position until I get stopped out, so I can know that I traded the stock properly from start to finish. It is always disappointing to sell for a small profit and then see a stock run without you. I do not turn momentum trades into swing trades, because when a stock is up 20-30% intraday, it is usually not a good idea to hold overnight. Sometimes they will continue running, but the risk is too high to justify the reward.

Exit Indicators

If I see any of the following exit indicators, I immediately exit my position:

1. A five minute candle making a new low BEFORE I have scaled out of half my position (five minute candles making a new low can indicate a possible reversal)

2. Price breaks below the 9 EMA on the five minute chart

3. I adjusted my stop to breakeven and get stopped out

When I am trading momentum, I have learned to follow a handful of reliable exit indicators. If I am in a trade and I see an exit indicator, I immediately close my position, regardless of the total profit or loss. I have found that waiting for my stop to hit after seeing an exit indicator will only serve to make the loss bigger. The goal of trading is to cap our losses. That means as soon as a trade gives you a reason to exit, you take the hint and move on to the next opportunity.

The first exit indicator is a five minute candle making a new low, before I have scaled out of half my position. Once I am in the driver's seat and have sold half my position, and adjusted my stop to breakeven, I am willing to hold through a five minute candle making a new low. I may end up holding through the formation of a second bull flag and be able to ride the momentum. As long as the price does not come back down to my entry price, I can stay in the position.

The second exit indicator is the price breaking below the 9 EMA. Regardless of whether I have scaled out or I am holding my full position, if the price breaks below the 9 EMA, I have to exit the trade and take whatever profit or loss I have. I use the 9 EMA to gauge the strength of the trend. Strong momentum stocks will trend along the 9 EMA, making moves up and away, and then consolidating back down near the moving average. Stocks can run all day long without breaking the 9 EMA. By using a break of the 9 EMA as my final exit indicator, I have the potential of holding a partial position for hours while a stock continues to run. This is how big winners are made.

The final indicator is if my stop price is triggered. My stop price should have initially been based on either my maximum loss or a specific support level. As the trade progresses, I adjust my stops first to breakeven, and then into the profit zone. By holding that final position until my stop fired, it ensured I have traded the full range without selling too soon.

CHAPTER 9

COUNTER TREND (REVERSAL) TRADING STRATEGIES

In addition to trading momentum stocks to the upside, I am a big fan of trading reversals. One of the first things I realized as a new trader was that, it is impossible to predict when a stock is going to make a big move to the upside or the downside, but almost all of those moves will result in a reversal. Instead of feeling frustrated that I missed a big mover, I saw it as an opportunity to trade the reversal. The challenge is finding the reversal and not getting in a stock going the wrong direction too early. Many counter trend traders experience large losses, because they start entering reversal positions too soon. Since countertrend trading requires guessing the change in trend, it is naturally more difficult than momentum trading. The big advantage of reversal trading is that when you buy a weak stock very close to the bottom, you will have an amazing profit loss ratio. The risk is almost always very low relative to the profit potential, because your stop is at the high of day or low of day. We already learned having a 2:1 profit loss ratio means you can be a profitable trader with just 50% success rate. On reversal trades, I often get 3:1 profit loss ratios. I will have a 10-15 cent stop at the low of day and get 50 cents of profit off the bounce. These types of profit loss ratios mean even if the accuracy rate is lower, you can afford to take more losses since the winners will generally far outweigh the losers.

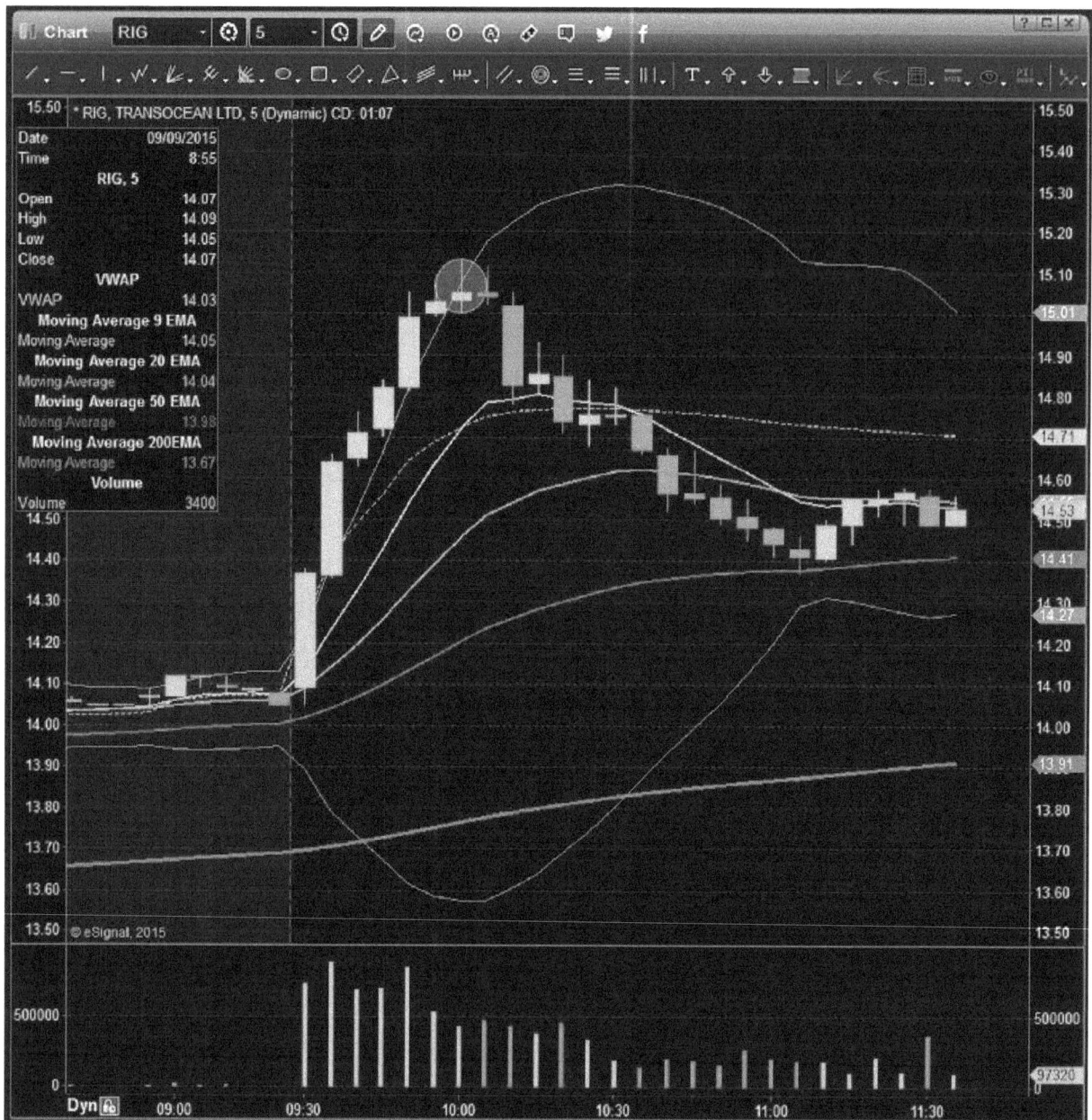

Counter Trend Trading Chart.

One of the big questions students will ask is, how I'm able to determine if a stock has the potential to make a big bounce. I will answer this with an example. Think of a rubber band, when the rubber band gets extremely stretched out, it will snap back with tremendous force. Applying that concept to trading, we need to look for stocks that are extremely extended to the upside or the downside. The biggest mistakes students make is underestimating how extreme the extension needs to be.

Only Trading Extremes

Reversal setups need to be either at high of day or low of day, with at least 3-5 consecutive long body candles, although 5-10 is preferable. The final candle in the string of consecutive candles should be a candle outside the bollinger bands. A candle outside the bollinger bands is a definitive indicator of an extreme move. Additionally, I look for the Relative Strength Index to show the stock is either above 80 (overbought) or below 20 (oversold). I require more indicators than a momentum trade, because reversals are difficult to time properly.

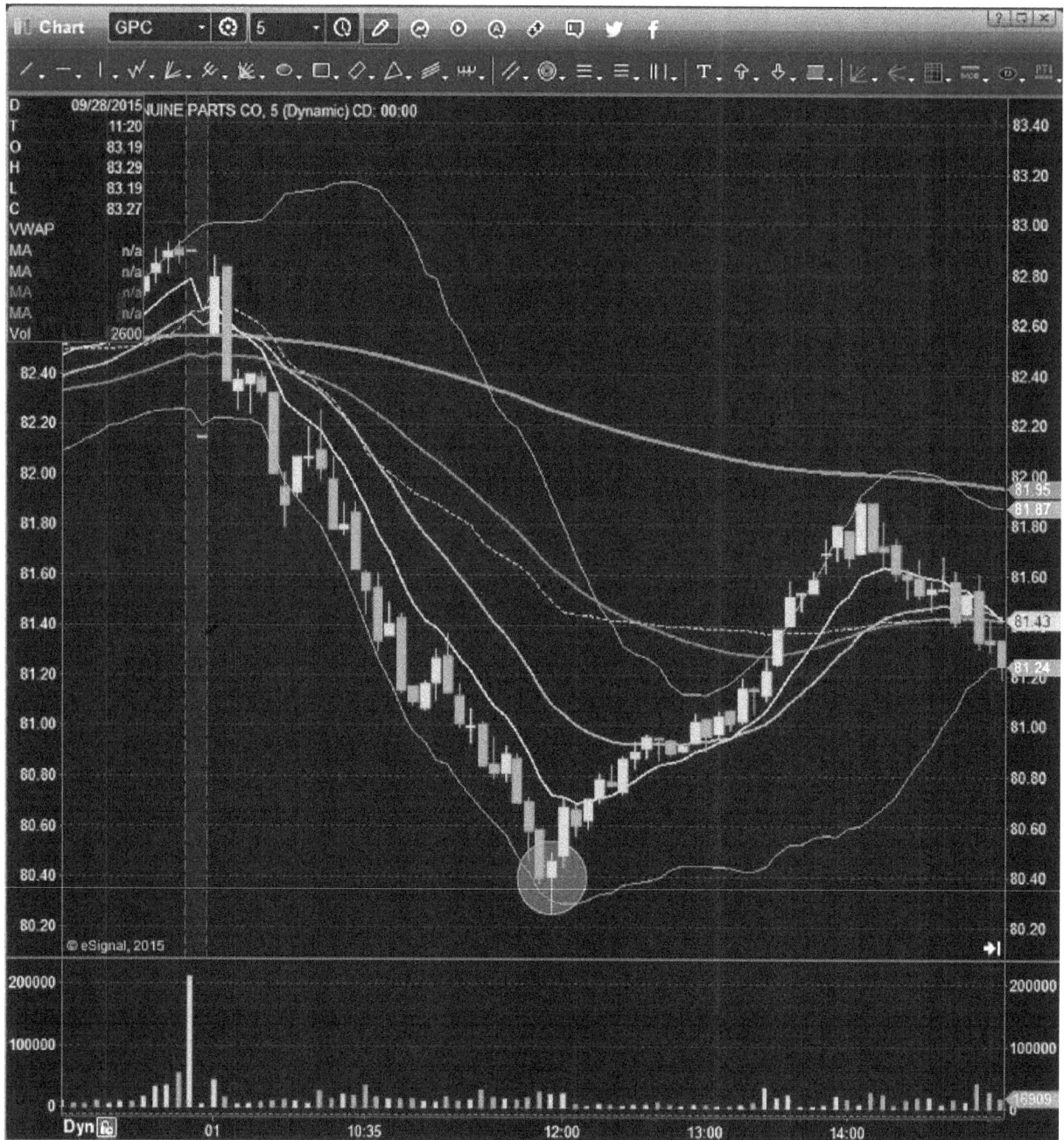

Chart showing Reversal Bar at the bottom of the downtrend.

The Reversal Bar

The last candle in the series will be our reversal bar. The best reversal bar will be fully outside the bollinger bands, and should ideally take the form of a doji, a topping or bottoming tail, or a hammer or inverted hammer. That candlestick becomes our trigger candle that we will use to base our entry and stop price. In the case of a top reversal, we will short the first five minute candle to make a new low, versus the low of the trigger candle. Our stop will be the high of the trigger candle. I have to adjust my size based on the level of risk between my entry and the stop price.

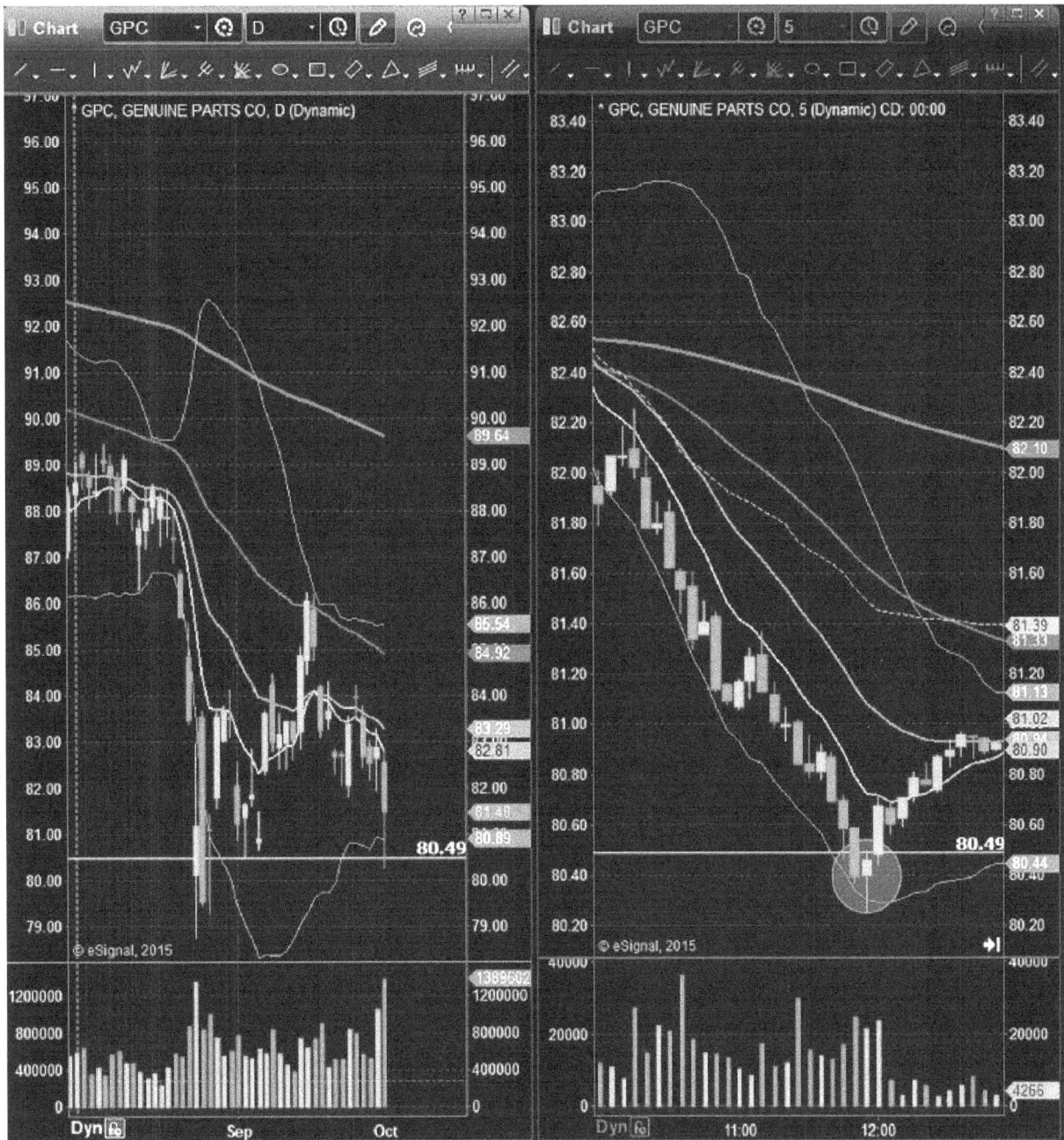

Chart showing five minute bottom bounce alignment with a daily support level.

Alignment with the Daily Chart

Although countertrend trades can be profitable without running into support or resistance on the daily chart, many of the best reversal setups will have confirmation on the daily chart. The daily confirmation helps justifying the reversal point, which means more traders will participate in the reversal trade. As we know from our lesson earlier, more volume generally means better resolution. The reversal point on the daily chart can be touching a critical area of support or resistance, or running into a moving average. The obvious daily levels will typically provide more support than obscure levels.

Volume

Although volume is not as important on reversals as it is on momentum trades, I still prefer to see high relative volume. Some of the best reversal trades will experience the highest volume of the day on the last candle, before the reversal. When this occurs, it is called a volume top or a volume bottom. On momentum trades, we need the high volume in order for the breakout to happen. With reversal trades, if the tide changes after an extreme sell off, the stock can grind back up toward the VWAP on lighter volume. As a general rule of thumb, I need to see at least 500,000 in volume on the day, in order to consider a reversal trade. When we trade reversals on lighter volume, we need to be especially aware of the influence of the overall market. When the overall market is very weak, a lot of stocks will show up as potential reversal candidates, because they are selling off in sympathy with the market. If the market does indeed bounce, these stocks will often bounce nicely, but if the market keeps selling, it will pull those stocks back down.

Sector Extremes

There are times when an entire sector is very extended to the upside or the downside. Stocks that show up on our reversal scanner will meet the technical requirements for a reversal, but may not always be appropriate for trading. During a day when an entire sector is weak, we have to be careful taking reversal trades. However, if the overall sector begins to reverse, any of the stocks on the reversal scanner can be traded because out of the hundreds of stocks in the sector, those stocks met our requirements the best. Often times I will pick several stocks in the same sector on the scanner, and try to catch a sector wide reversal across several different stocks. Even though the sector is reversing, some stocks will reverse with more strength than others.

Reversal Entry Requirements

1. 3+ Consecutive five minute candles

2. Candles are riding the bollinger bands or outside the bollinger bands

3. Stock is at High of Day or Low of Day

4. RSI is above 80 or below 20

5. Float is typically not an issue here, but is worth noting before entering a position

6. Ideally, the final candle is one of our preferred reversal candles

7. Ideally, we are bouncing off daily resistance

8. Ideally, the overall market supports our decision

9. I must be able to reasonably achieve a 2:1 profit loss ratio

10. There must be at least 30 cents to the 9 EMA on the five minute chart

Entering a Reversal Trade

When I am preparing to enter a reversal trade, I pull up the Level2 and look at the spreads (the distance between the Bid and the Ask), and review the level of volume. If the stock meets all my entry requirements, I will take a position and immediately put out either a 20 cent stop or a stop at the high or low of day. I typically start a reversal trade with quarter or half size positions. Like parabolic trades, I may have the right idea, but the wrong timing. By starting with smaller size I can allow a little bit more room for the stock to move before stopping me out at my maximum loss. If a stock does break to a new high or new low I will exit, but as long as the price is between my entry and the stop, I will hold on.

One Minute Entry

I often take my first quarter size position based on the first one minute candle to make a new high, if there is a series of at least 10 consecutive one minute candles. I always try to enter a reversal trade with the first position based on the one minute chart, and then if I am profitable, and when we get five minute confirmation, I will double my position to full size. Looking at the one minute chart, if I see the stock touching a level of daily resistance, I may decide to take my first position before the five minute confirmation. Since we know stocks run into support and resistance around whole dollars and half dollars, I will sometimes look to buy a weak stock if I see it break below a whole dollar, such as $50.00. I will then buy it if it comes back up through that whole dollar. If it can reclaim the support of the whole dollar, that is often a safe entry with a stop at $49.90. In the case of a strong stock surging up, if the stock breaks through a price such as $50.00, I will short it as it breaks back down below the whole dollar, with a stop at $50.10. These one minute entries can give me a great average very close to the high of day or low of day, but I will be ready to bail out if the reversal does not hold. Since it is riskier to trade reversals on the one minute chart, I use smaller size until we have a five minute confirmation. Beginner traders may be wise to avoid trading reversals on the one minute chart, and instead use the five minute.

Five Minute Entry

The five minute entry is very simple. Reversal confirmation is a candle over candle pattern on the five minute chart. When we have a candle outside the bollinger bands on the five minute chart, I use the bottom of that candle as my stop and the top of that candle as either my entry point or my double up point. I will only take this trade if there is still 30 cents of profit potential to the 9 EMA, using the five minute chart. If I already have a half sized position based on the one minute chart, I will double on five minute confirmation. When I double my position, I am increasing my risk, that means I need to tighten up my stop to either break even or -10 cents. It's important to watch the one minute chart when you enter a five minute reversal. If there have already been five consecutive green candles on the five minute chart, there is a risk that you may be chasing the reversal too much.

Chart showing a one minute candle making a new high several times (1), when this happens we need to wait for consolidation above the lows (2) and then finally a break of the high of the consolidation (3). Until we have (3) there is no entry.

Buying the First Pullback of Reversals

One of the safest reversal strategies is buying the first pullback after confirmation. There are times when the one minute or five minute chart is too choppy during a downtrend to take a position on the first candle to make a new high. In this case, there are two options. One is to simply pass on the reversal and wait for a better opportunity, and this may be a good option for new traders who prefer stronger confirmation before entering trades. My preferred technique is to buy the first pullback on the one minute chart or the five minute chart. In the example of AVGO, you can see that the one minute chart showed several one minute candles making a new high. If you took each of those trades, you would have had four back to back losses until you hit a winner. In the section where we discussed one minute entries, we emphasized the importance of at least 5-10 consecutive candles, which AVGO did not have. In this type of situation, I keep reversal stocks on watch and wait for the one minute or five minute candle to make a new high (1), and then consolidate above the lows showing that support has been found (2), and then finally break the high of the consolidation (3). I enter at step (3), with a stop at the bottom of the consolidation. This entry provides the best balance of a tight stop and confirmation that the reversal is beginning. In the example of AVGO, the point where we saw the breakout from the consolidation coincided almost perfectly with the first five minute candle making a new high. AVGO also showed (3), as being the first time the one minute candle broke the 20 EMA, since the selloff began. When I am looking for pullback opportunities on reversal trades, I use the same stock scanners as when I am looking for the first one minute or five minute candles to make a new high.

Profit Targets

Reversal trades have obvious profit targets. Unlike a momentum trade which can run and run, reversal trades usually run back to logical points on the chart. I look for reversals to come back to the 9 EMA, on the five minute chart. A strong reversal could get back to the VWAP, and potentially cross over the VWAP. Since the 9 EMA is the first profit target, I will not take a trade if I cannot get at least a 2:1 profit loss ratio, based on an exit at the 9 EMA.

Exit Indicators

1. When I first enter a reversal trade, I set my stop either at the high of day or low of day. If my stop gets touched, I am immediately out of the trade.

2. I will sell half when the price touches the 9 EMA on the five minute chart, or when I hit my 2:1 profit loss ratio. I then adjust my stop to breakeven on the balance.

3. Once the price breaks the 9 EMA, I will adjust my stop to the other side of the 9 EMA, and keep adjusting it every 5-10 minutes.

4. At the VWAP, I will do another partial sell and keep a smaller position for a move back over the VWAP and for a possible swing trade.

I am very quick to exit reversal trades when they are not looking strong. If anything, I may jump out of them too quickly sometimes. One of the things I have noticed is, that with reversal trades, since we are expecting that rubber band snap back effect, it needs to happen almost immediately. The stock may not be moving against me, but the fact that it is not moving up is a big warning sign. Just like my momentum trades, typically my best reversal trades work almost immediately. Sometimes reversal trades will pause near the high or low, before making a big surge and continuing in the direction of the trend. This means instead of holding out hope that maybe the reversal will work, it is much better to get out breakeven, or for a small loss instead of experiencing the pain of it ripping against you.

I will warn you against the bad habit of covering a reversal position and flipping directions by jumping in for a momentum trade. Reversal setups are rarely momentum setups. They are reversal setups because they are extremely extended. This means even if they run another 50 cents, they are in an extremely extended position and the reversal will come sooner or later. Trading the trend when the 'rubber band' is stretched, is asking for trouble. If you bail out of the reversal position, jump into the momentum, and then the snap back happens and you lose on both sides, you will feel extremely frustrated. Anytime I get stopped on my first try on a reversal, I simply wait for a better reversal opportunity. If the stock keeps running, that means the extension will be bigger and the snapback potential will be stronger as well.

CHAPTER 10

STOCK SCANNING & BUILDING A WATCH LIST

I find almost every single trade setup on one of my stock scanners. I use stock scanning software provided by Trade-Ideas (www.trade-ideas.com). I cannot speak highly enough about their tools. Without their scanning software, I would be lost as a trader. A trader can have all the textbook knowledge of the markets, but if they are unable to find setups in real-time, they will never be profitable. Stock scanners are the tools we use to find tradable setups. Before stock scanners existed, traders would trade off a master watch list of their top 50 stocks, or wait for news to break over the wire about a particular stock. This is not an effective method of day trading because out of the several thousand stocks available to trade, typically there are only 5-10 stocks in play each day. I consider a stock in play if it is surging up or down more than 4%, with a strong catalyst. Using stock scanners, I can choose the specific type of stocks I want to see and filter out all the noise. This adds tremendous clarity to my stock selection process. I can also make complex scanners to look for specific chart patterns, or I can use simple scanners to look for broad matches such as stocks that just reported earnings in the last 24hrs.

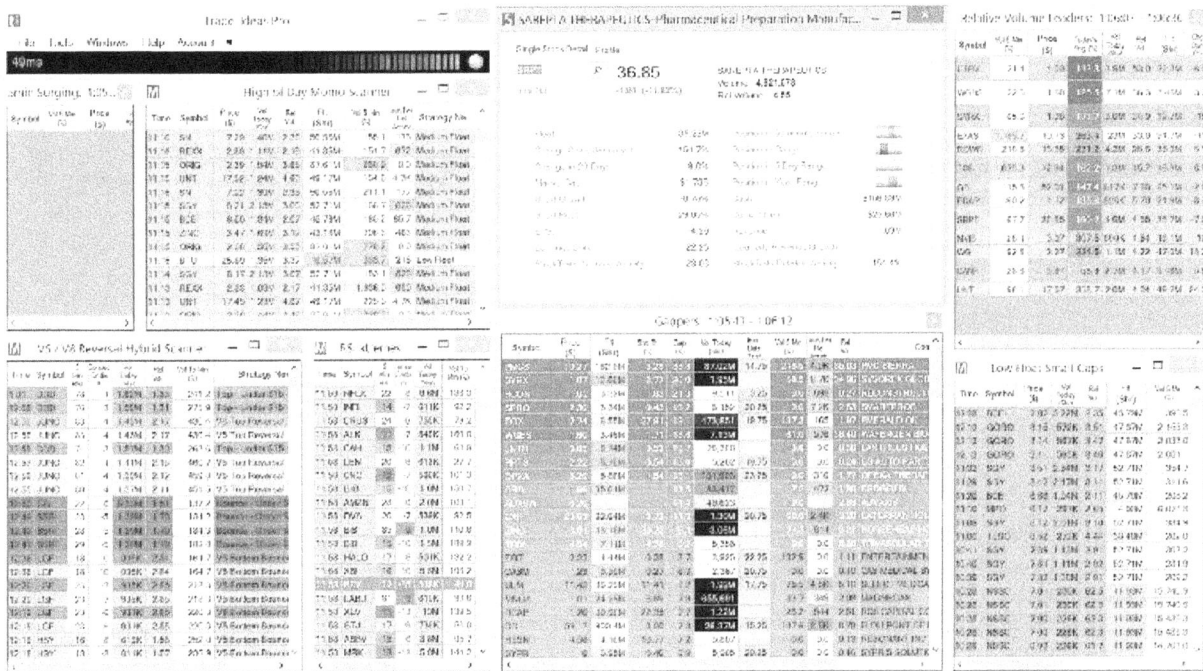

Full Scanner Layout by Trade-Ideas

Day trading is a very difficult career that we can make a little easier by using the best tools. This includes stock scanners. One of the great features of Trade-Ideas is the ability to view historical data of a stock scan. I can look back and see all the alerts from a day or week, and review the results. This saves us a tremendous amount of time sitting and watching scanners in real-time to develop a back test history. We can instantly back test and quickly correct inconsistencies or false alert issues. I provide all of the students in our live trading courses with the proprietary stock scanner settings I have developed over the years. Students are able to use the exact same tools I use every day to find trades. Although I have about 15 scanners I am actively using every day, they are clustered between two groups. I have scanners looking for reversal opportunities and I have scanners looking for momentum trades. Those are the two strategies I trade and those are the setup ideas I need to find those trades in real-time. All of the stock scanners I use have been highly customized to provide me with a watch list of the type of stocks I have the highest percentage of success trading.

Gappers: 8:48:35 - 8:49:04

Symbol	Price (S)	Flt (Shr)	Shrt Ft (%)	Gap (%)	Vol Today (Shr)	Earn Date (Due)	Vol 5 Min (%)	ock Twn Rel Activity	Rel Vol	Company Name
PSTI	2.62	67.04M	1.01	24.8	100	-1.50	0.0	0.0		PLURISTEM THERAPEUTIC
PGI	13.86	39.93M	1.75	22.1	38,976		199.8	6.6K		PREMIERE GLOBAL SERVICES
ARWR	8.32	58.91M	27.14	10.5	24,171		64.8	530		ARROWHEAD RESEARCH
OLLI	20.00	16.51M	5.80	9.6	100	-1.25	0.0	0.0		OLLIES BARGAIN OUTLET HOLDINGS
NXTD	1.20	9.84M	2.97	8.1	100		0.0	0.0		NXT-ID
VVUS	1.63	85.82M	38.90	5.2	82,760		21.1	840		VIVUS
ZSPH	78.50	17.45M	16.93	5.0	17,390		1.9	2.1K		ZS PHARMA
EDAP	4.40	24.91M		5.0	1,500	-11.25	0.0	663		EDAP TMS SA
ADXS	16.67	22.50M	34.35	4.4	4,673		0.0	699		ADVAXIS
AERI	18.32	20.87M	26.66	4.2	200		0.0	269		AERIE PHARMACEUTICALS
CBPX	20.10	31.53M	3.26	-6.0	17,050		55.4	7.0K		CONTINENTAL BUILDING PRODUCTS
BRC	19.90	47.39M	5.84	-7.5	405	0.25	0.0	9.4K		BRADY
WCIC	22.79	19.17M	4.24	-10.2	1,874		0.0	1.3K		WCI COMMUNITIES INC
MFRM	52.79	15.16M	27.99	-12.5	18,938	0.25	5.8	10K		MATTRESS FIRM HOLDINGS
FNSR	12.55	102.9M	10.21	-15.8	52,982	-0.25	19.3	5.3K		FINISAR
MRVL	8.41	445.3M	1.91	-20.3	1.06M	-15.75	254.2	2.0K		MARVELL TECH
ZUMZ	17.25	21.76M	13.81	-20.4	105,497	-0.25	73.2	5.5K		ZUMIEZ
EFOI	17.60	3.26M	2.00	-23.5	229,847		217.6	557		ENERGY FOCUS INC
CHKE	16.00	6.55M	3.45	-33.6	3,550	-0.25	25.9	5.5K		CHEROKEE

Image of Gap Scanner by Trade-Ideas.

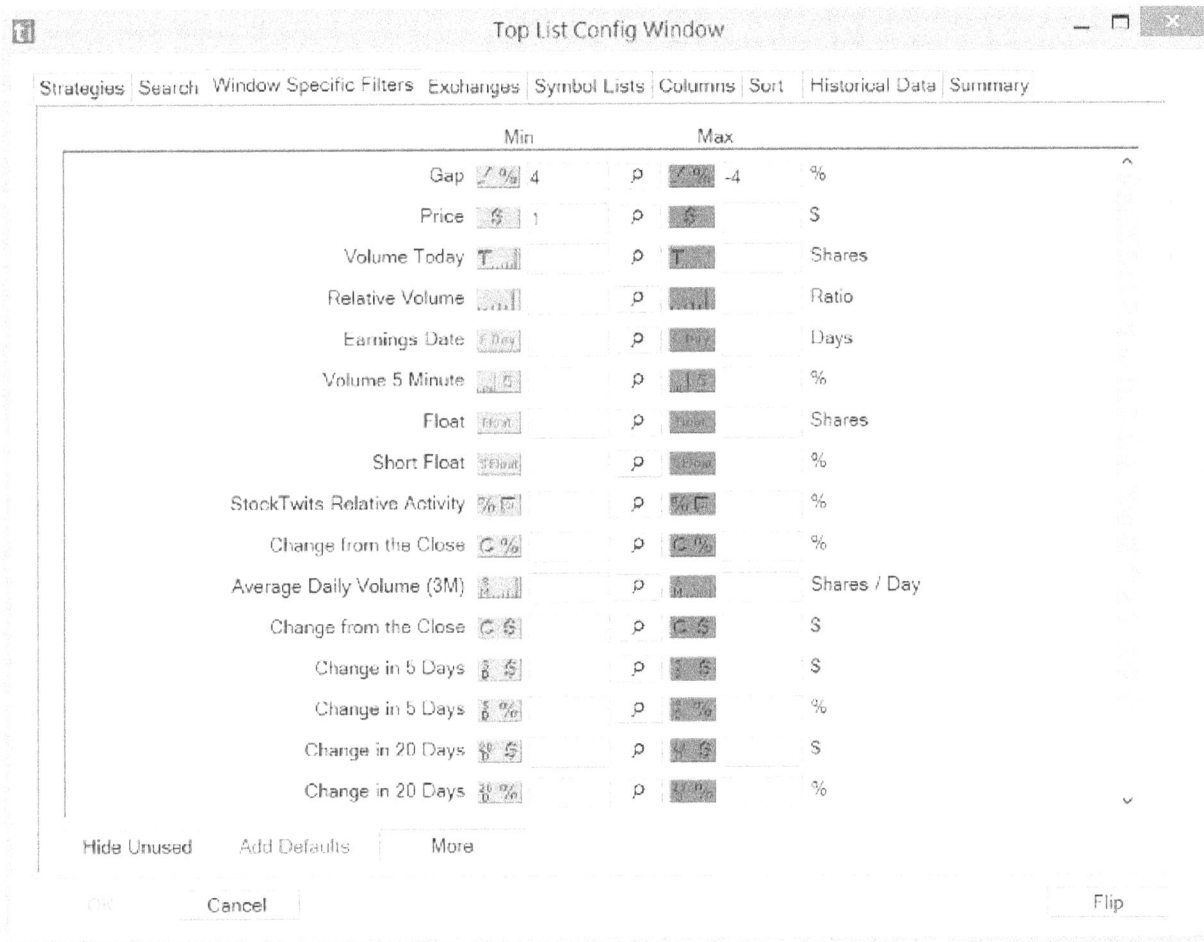

	Min			Max	
Gap	⌀ % 4	ρ	⌀ % -4	%	
Price	$ 1	ρ	$	$	
Volume Today	T	ρ	T	Shares	
Relative Volume		ρ		Ratio	
Earnings Date	Day	ρ	Day	Days	
Volume 5 Minute	5	ρ	5	%	
Float	Float	ρ	Float	Shares	
Short Float	Float	ρ	Float	%	
StockTwits Relative Activity	%	ρ	%	%	
Change from the Close	C %	ρ	C %	%	
Average Daily Volume (3M)	M	ρ	M	Shares / Day	
Change from the Close	C $	ρ	C $	$	
Change in 5 Days	$	ρ	$	$	
Change in 5 Days	%	ρ	%	%	
Change in 20 Days	$	ρ	$	$	
Change in 20 Days	%	ρ	%	%	

Hide Unused   Add Defaults   More

OK   Cancel   Flip

Gap Scanner Settings.

Gap Scanners

The first thing I do every morning is check my gap scanner. This shows me the list of stocks gapping up or down more than 4%. I sort the results on the gap scanners by biggest percentage of gap, then largest volume. I switch sorting methods to find the most active stocks each morning. As traders we have to follow the volume, so I always put a special emphasis on the amount of pre-market volume.

Creating your Pre-Market Watch List

It is critical to your success as a trader, that you are able to make a watch list each day. Your watch list will be a list of the top 4-6 stocks each day, that have the potential to make 5-10% intraday moves. By 9

AM, I have built a watch list of the top 4-6 stocks I think will be in play each day. These will be stocks already trading on heavy pre-market volume due to a catalyst. I find these stocks using simple stock scanners that are displayed in our day trading chat room. For each of the stocks on my watch list, I take notes about the catalyst, float, key price levels on the daily chart that are in play and potential entry points. It is important to keep a close eye on the stocks you put on your daily watch list, because you know if a pattern forms you will not miss it. Many new students jump from chart to chart during the day, and end up missing all the setups because they never focused on one stock long enough to see a pattern. The best approach is to keep your favorite watch list stocks on the radar all day long, while looking at other stocks on a separate screen.

Once you get into the habit of creating a watch list of stocks every day, you are well on your way to becoming a trader! In order to trade, you need to find stocks worth trading. This means building a watch list every day and then reviewing how each of the stocks off your watch list performed. Sometimes, a great looking pre-market candidate will end up being out of play, because of a rapid morning sell off. Other times, a stock that was not on your watch list at all, will become the biggest mover of the day.

High of Day Momo Scanner

Time	Symbol	Price ($)	Vol Today (Shr)	Rel Vol	Flt (Shr)	Vol 5 Min (%)	ockTwi Rel Actvty	Strategy Na...	Today's Rng (%)
9:30	AQXP	19.33	1.97M	6.7K	4.51M	464.6	3.2K	Daily Breakout	202
9:30	AQXP	19.30	1.97M	6.7K	4.51M	460.7	3.2K	Daily Breakout	199
9:30	AQXP	19.21	1.97M	6.7K	4.51M	459.3	3.2K	Daily Breakout	188
9:30	AQXP	19.11	1.96M	6.7K	4.51M	455.0	3.2K	Daily Breakout	177
9:30	AQXP	18.98	1.96M	6.9K	4.51M	444.2	3.2K	Daily Breakout	162
9:30	AQXP	18.93	1.96M	6.9K	4.51M	443.9	3.2K	Daily Breakout	156
9:30	AQXP	19.38	1.99M	6.6K	4.51M	486.0	3.2K	Low Float	208
9:30	AQXP	19.33	1.97M	6.7K	4.51M	464.6	3.2K	Low Float	202
9:30	AQXP	19.30	1.97M	6.7K	4.51M	460.7	3.2K	Low Float	199
9:30	AQXP	19.21	1.97M	6.7K	4.51M	459.3	3.2K	Low Float	188
9:30	AQXP	19.11	1.96M	6.7K	4.51M	455.0	3.2K	Low Float	177
9:30	AQXP	18.98	1.96M	6.9K	4.51M	444.2	3.2K	Low Float	162
9:30	AQXP	18.93	1.96M	6.9K	4.51M	443.9	3.2K	Low Float	156
9:30	AQXP	18.87	1.95M	6.8K	4.51M	433.9	3.2K	Low Float	149
9:30	VLTC	10.10	467K	125	2.21M	982.7	528	Low Float	60.6
9:30	VLTC	9.90	372K	2.9K	2.21M	407.6	528	Low Float	19.5
9:30	VLTC	9.75	371K	2.9K	2.21M	402.7	528	Low Float	3.2

Image of Momentum Scanner by Trade-Ideas.

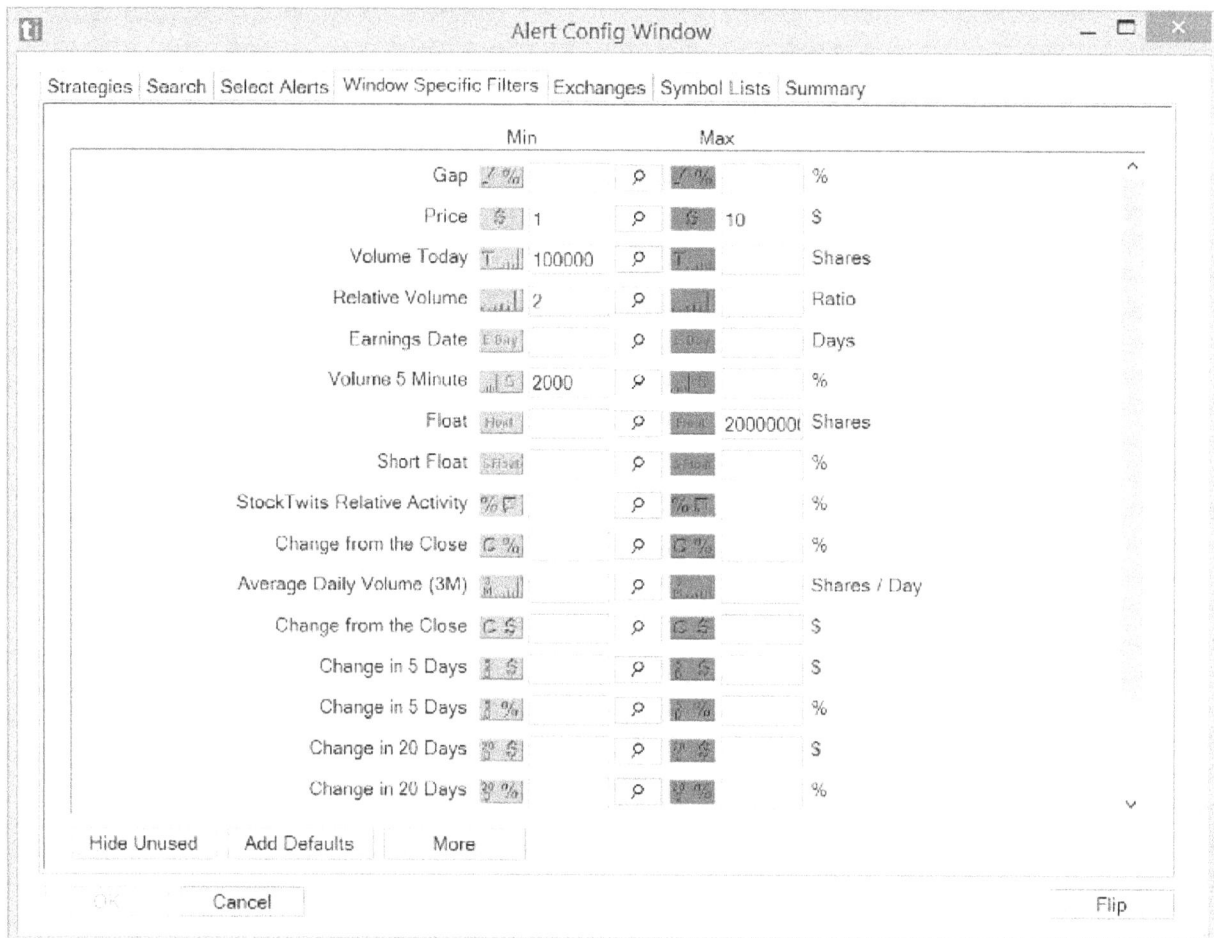

Alert Config Window

Strategies | Search | Select Alerts | Window Specific Filters | Exchanges | Symbol Lists | Summary

	Min		Max	
Gap		🔍		%
Price	$ 1	🔍	$ 10	$
Volume Today	100000	🔍		Shares
Relative Volume	2	🔍		Ratio
Earnings Date		🔍		Days
Volume 5 Minute	2000	🔍		%
Float		🔍	20000000	Shares
Short Float		🔍		%
StockTwits Relative Activity		🔍		%
Change from the Close		🔍		%
Average Daily Volume (3M)		🔍		Shares / Day
Change from the Close		🔍		$
Change in 5 Days		🔍		$
Change in 5 Days		🔍		%
Change in 20 Days		🔍		$
Change in 20 Days		🔍		%

Hide Unused | Add Defaults | More

OK | Cancel | Flip

Momentum Scanner Settings.

Momentum Scanners

I use this same process for writing a scanner to look for momentum stocks. The important filter for momentum stocks is the high relative volume and the 15 minute volume surge. By turning up these minimum filters, I can see the most active stocks in the market each day. All scanners produce some false alerts, which is why we cannot trade solely based on the alerts of a stock scanner. I have momentum scanners looking for stocks experiencing 52 week highs, daily chart breakouts, massive intraday volume and extreme rate of change. Anytime I see a stock show up on one of my momentum scanners, I can immediately begin to review the chart for windows and triggers and look to apply a Momentum Trading Strategy setup.

Some of the best momentum scanner alerts will be stocks that were not even on our watch list, which was based on pre-market volume. Breaking news released in the middle of the day can cause a stock to suddenly come into play. When this is the case, we have to make a quick analysis of the catalyst and the level of risk involved in the potential trade. Taking a spontaneous midday trade can result in unexpected losses if we do not first consider the risk. Anytime a stock begins to spike or move quickly on breaking news, I like to watch it and let the dust settle before taking any trades. Sometimes prices will spike up and then come right back down in a matter of minutes. If the news is legitimate, and the stock continues to trade on heavy volume, it is worth adding to the watch list. Remember that it is important to confirm the source of any breaking news story before entering a trade. We can apply the Momentum Trading Strategy and possibly the Reversal Trading Strategies to breaking news setups. Typically, stocks that spike up in the middle of the day on news, will be worth watching for the rest of the day because they will trade on high relative volume.

V5 / V8 Reversal Hybrid Scanner

Time	Symbol	5 Min RSI (0 - 100)	Consec Cndls (5	Vol Today (Shr)	Rel Vol	Vol 15 Min (%)	Pos Bol Bnd	Strategy Na
11:40	CONN	75.2	7	671K	3.00	198.0	118	V8 Top Rever
11:40	CONN	75.2	7	671K	3.00	198.0	118	V5 Top Rever
11:38	CONN	74.0	6	655K	2.96	206.2	131	V8 Top Rever
11:38	CONN	74.0	6	655K	2.96	206.2	131	V5 Top Rever
11:38	SGEN	71.6	5	3.17M	12.85	524.9	101	V8 Top Rever
11:38	SGEN	71.6	5	3.17M	12.85	524.9	101	V5 Top Rever
11:24	ANET	13.2	-12	865K	4.65	777.4	-10	V8 Bottom Bo
11:24	ANET	13.2	-12	865K	4.65	777.4	-10	V5 Bottom Bo
11:23	ANET	14.5	-12	848K	4.60	723.5	-1.8	V8 Bottom Bo
11:23	ANET	14.5	-12	848K	4.60	723.5	-1.8	V5 Bottom Bo
11:18	ANET	14.7	-11	811K	4.53	724.4	-7.2	V8 Bottom Bo
11:18	ANET	14.7	-11	811K	4.53	724.4	-7.2	V5 Bottom Bo
11:17	ANET	16.2	-11	776K	4.37	607.3	1.6	V5 Bottom Bo
11:16	ANET	16.3	-11	760K	4.33	555.0	2.1	V5 Bottom Bo
11:15	ANET	17.1	-11	733K	4.21	471.8	6.2	V5 Bottom Bo
11:11	ANET	17.2	-10	698K	4.11	472.4	0.2	V5 Bottom Bo

Image of Reversal Scanner by Trade-Ideas.

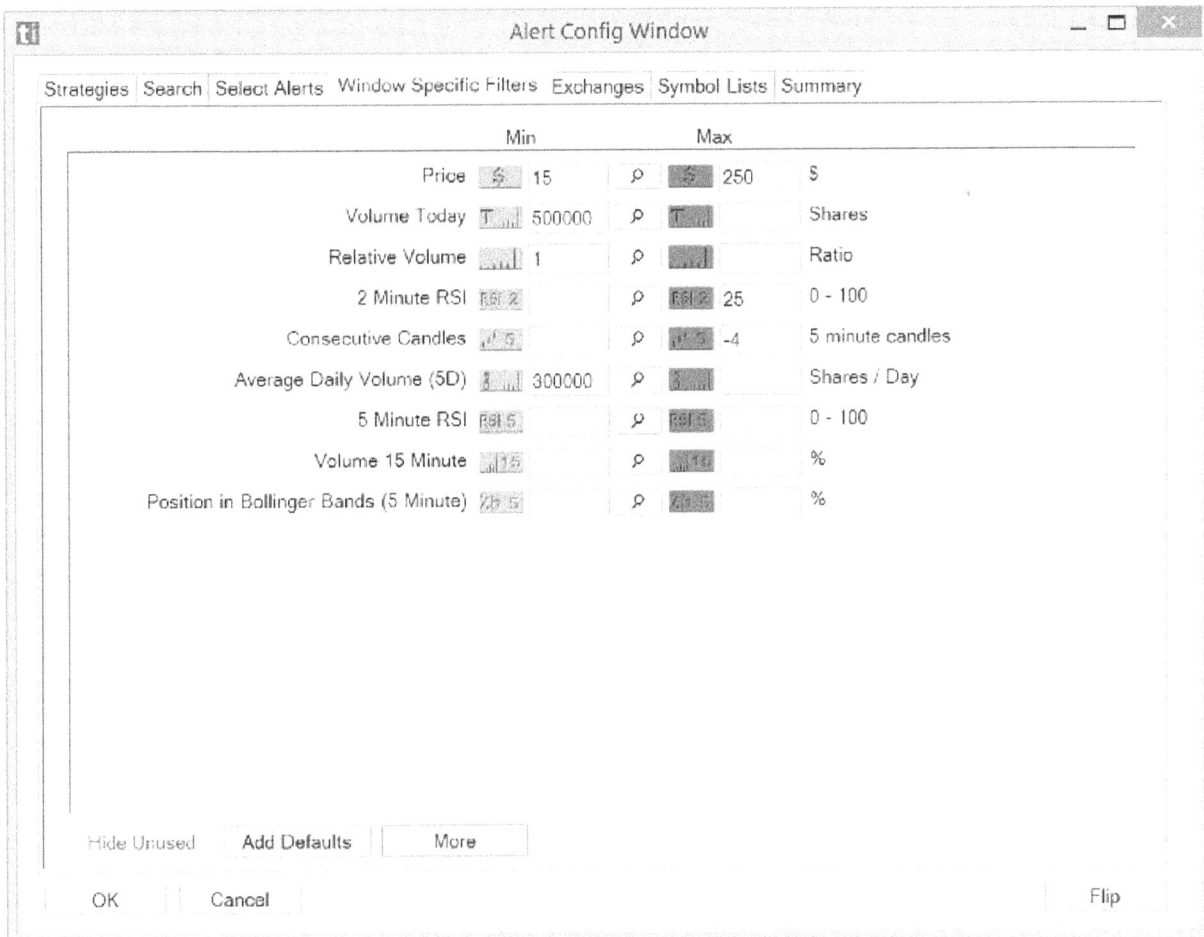

	Min		Max		
Price	$ 15	ρ	$ 250		$
Volume Today	T 500000	ρ	T		Shares
Relative Volume	1	ρ			Ratio
2 Minute RSI	RSI 2	ρ	RSI 2 25		0 - 100
Consecutive Candles	5	ρ	5 -4		5 minute candles
Average Daily Volume (5D)	300000	ρ			Shares / Day
5 Minute RSI	RSI 5	ρ	RSI 5		0 - 100
Volume 15 Minute	15	ρ	15		%
Position in Bollinger Bands (5 Minute)	5	ρ			%

Hide Unused   Add Defaults   More

OK   Cancel   Flip

Reversal Scanner Settings.

Reversal Scanners

I write a stock scanner to look for a specific type of setup. That means I need to dissect the setup and understand all of its features that make it unique. For reversal trades, I set a minimum volume filter of 500,000 shares, a price filter of $15-250, and a consecutive candle filter of at least 4 (consecutive trending candles). I know the best reversal trades have these characteristics in common. I then begin adding settings for RSI (Relative Strength Index), position within bollinger bands and percentage of change today. After fine tuning the settings, the end result is a scanner that shows me stocks at any given time of the day, that match my exact entry conditions for a reversal trade.

CHAPTER 11

THREE STEP DAY TRADING PLAN

In our live trading courses, we put our students on a three step trading plan, and meet with them twice a week to review their progress. It is extremely important that students trade in a simulated and closely monitored environment during their first months of trading. We want to see the mistakes our students are making, so we can quickly address and correct bad habits. All students make mistakes learning to trade. That is part of the learning process. We have students trading in a simulated environment, so their inevitable losses and beginner mistakes do not come with a price tag attached. During the first few months of trading, some students will also realize that the level of risk involved in day trading is not suitable for them. We encourage an honest reflection of your experience as a trader. Day trading can be stressful, and dealing with financial loss on a nearly daily basis is not for everyone.

The ability to day trade as your primary source of income, is not a skill that is learned overnight. It takes thousands of hours of practice, training and studying. Like almost any other profession, mastery comes with time. The challenge for many students is, that they make mistakes in their first few months of trading, blow up their accounts and give up before they ever really had a chance to succeed. The failure to manage risk and the tendency to live trade unproven strategies generally results in career ending blow ups. We want to prevent our students from having that painful experience. It will be rare to find a professional trader who does not have a horror story of big losses and big mistakes, we all have them. The difference between traders that give up and those that keep on fighting through, is often a matter of financial resources. Our goal is for you to trade in a simulated environment, until you have proven you can be profitable. By the end of our three step trading plan, you will have refined your strategies and developed a sense of emotional composure that will allow you to trade through the ups and downs, without losing focus.

It is important to set realistic expectations before you start your trading plan. Expect that in your first six months, you are unlikely to produce substantial profits. Instead, you are taking the steps necessary to build a foundation for your future growth as a trader. Many traders will try to skip steps and end up making costly mistakes that will jeopardize their ability to continue trading. Remember, that every single trade you take will give you a little bit more experience and a better understanding of the market. For that reason, the longer you are able to survive in the market breaking even, or just treading water with small profits, the greater your odds for success. You have to survive until your thrive.

Three Step Trading Plan

During the first month in our trading plan, you will begin each morning with 30 minutes of aerobic exercise. You will be doing this Monday-Friday, for the next three months. It is really important for our students to focus on the emotional conditioning required to make the right decisions under pressure, and exercise has been proven to help sharpen the mind. Every morning when I am exercising, I remind myself I am doing this so I can be the best trader possible. Keeping the bigger picture in mind makes the workout go by faster.

Once you have finished your workout, the first thing you will do when you sit down at your desk is, look at the gap scan for the biggest gappers, and begin making a watch list of 4-6 stocks. You will write down the news catalyst associated with each stock and the entry prices and stop prices. If you are in our day trading chat room, you will see the breaking news headlines for all the big moving stocks. Typically, the headlines for all of the gappers will be posted by 9 AM. By 9:15 AM, your watch list should be prepared. This will be a list of Gap and Go candidates and possibly a couple of higher priced stocks that have a good catalyst, but will be too volatile for a Gap and Go trade. Between 9:15 AM and 9:30 AM, you will use your order entry window to prepare an order for each of the top four Gap and Go candidates. You will prepare your entry price based on rules of the Gap and Go Trading Strategy. When the market opens, and the trades begin to trigger at the pre-defined breakout spots, all you need to do is press the buy button and start managing your open positions. As the day progresses, you will watch the Momentum Scanners and the Reversal Scanners for trade opportunities.

During our three Step Trading Plan, you will take 10 trades a day. Some days you may take more than 10 trades, while other days you take fewer. The goal is to practice trading, experience the emotions of being in a position and managing the trade. Your trades should be based on Gap and Go Strategies, Momentum Trading Strategies, and Reversal Trading Strategies. It is extremely important that you track every single trade in a spreadsheet. We review the spreadsheets of our students in our live trading courses. We want to review accuracy rates, average winners versus average losers, and which strategy you trade the best. Your first month of trading is not about how much money you make, it is about learning which strategies are best suited for your personality, and discovering what type of trader you will be. In the second and third month, we will have you focus on the strategies you traded the best during your first month. As a day trader, you need to be a master of one strategy. Mastering one strategy will be key to your survival in the market, while you learn other strategies. Day trading is not a profession where you can succeed being a jack of all trades, but a master of none. You need to achieve a level of mastery with one strategy before adding another.

Step 1 in a Simulated Account - Month One

During your first month, you will be trading in a simulated environment. You will risk $50 per trade, with a max position size of 100 shares on stocks above $20, and a max position size of 200 shares on stocks below $20. You will take 10 trade each day with a goal of 50% success rate. Using a 2:1 profit loss ratio, we expect your winners will be $500 in total (5 trades x $100 profit per trade) and your losers will be $250 in total (5 trades x $50 loss per trade). This will leave you with a net profit of $250 per day. As a new trader, we do not expect you to achieve a full 2:1 profit loss ratio, and you may not even achieve 50% success in your first month. We want to be realistic and set your daily profit target at just $150 per day. This allows for mistakes and accounts for the possibility of small winners, while you test out the success of various strategies.

With a max loss of $50 per trade, you also must follow a daily max loss of $150. That means if you hit your full max loss on three trades in a row, you will have to shut down the platform for the day. This is an extremely important risk management technique. After we have hit our max loss, there is a high likelihood that our trading will become emotionally impaired. This is true even for me. I still follow a max loss, where I walk away at the end of the day. During your first month, we expect you will hit your $150 daily target four days out of the week, and one day you will hit your max loss. That means your weekly goal is your daily goal, multiplied by three, or $450 per week. These daily and weekly targets do not take into account commissions, since you are trading in a simulated environment.

By the end of your first month of trading, you have to review the statistics of your trading. It will be important to note your percentage of success overall, per strategy, by time of day and by price range. It will also be important to note your profit loss ratios. If you have been able to trade an average of 10 trades per day, you will have about 200 trades that you can analyze.

Success in your first month is defined not by total profits, but by your profit loss ratio and your percentage of success. The big question is, are your current statistics sustainable? Have you succeeded in capping losses at not more than $50 per trade? The most common struggles among our students in the first month is, a poor percentage of success. As long as you have a good profit loss ratio, we can work on improving your accuracy as you gain experience and learn to identify better setups. If you have successfully completed Step 1, you are ready to graduate to the next level. If not, you have to continue on the first month's trading plan, until you achieve better results. Students in our live trading courses meet with us twice a week to review their progress, discuss concerns and set goals for the upcoming trading sessions.

Step 1 in a Live Account - Month 2

Once you have completed a successful month in the simulated environment, you can consider switching to a live trading account. Some students spend several months in a simulated environment, before they achieve a level of success that they feel justified trading in a live account. Becoming a successful trader is not a process that can be rushed.

During your second month of the trading plan, you will take the data from your first month to make adjustments in your strategy. If you find an area of particular weakness, you will avoid that type of trading, whether it is a particular strategy, a price range or a certain time of day. We will have you focus instead, on the area where you are showing strength.

When you are ready to switch to a live trading account, you should repeat Step 1. This difference is, you will be trading with real money and you may find that the emotions of trading with real money change the experience. This may take some time to acclimate to. Once you have completed one month of successful trading in a live trading account, you are ready to graduate to Step 2 of our trading plan.

Step 2 - Month 3

You will continue to trade an average of 10 times a day, but now you will risk up to $100 per trade. Your max position size is now 200 shares on stocks over $20 and 400 shares on stocks under $20. Your daily profit target is $300, and your max daily loss is $300. You have a weekly goal of $900, your daily goal multiplied by three.

Throughout the third month, you should continue your exercise regimen and continue to track all of your trades in a spreadsheet. At the end of the month, you will review your performance and make adjustments as needed.

Step 3 - Month 4

In your final month of our trading plan, you will make more adjustments based on the performance of your previous month. As day traders, we are constantly making adjustments to our strategies and techniques in response to changing markets. Once you have developed a level of confidence in yourself and your abilities, you will simply flow from one strategy to another, based on greater market conditions. This is the ebb and flow of the markets that we have to respond to.

During month three, you will increase your risk per trade to $200. Your max position size will be 500 shares for stocks over $20, and 1000 shares for stocks under $20. Your daily profit target is $600 per day, with a weekly target of $1800 per week. Once you have completed our three Step Trading Plan successfully, you are on track to make just shy of $100,000 per year as a day trader. This is success. We teach day trading skills that can be used to generate income. We are not going to tell you that success comes overnight or that you can make a million dollars in your first year trading, but our students are proving that success is obtainable for those who work for it.

CONCLUSION

The frustrating reality that I am sure you know is, that success in trading will not come for most who try. With only 1 in 10 succeeding, the odds are stacked against us. We have addressed the primary reasons that most traders fail. They fail due to a lack of market education and a lack of risk management. These causes of failure are completely avoidable, and by spending your time reading this book, you are showing a level of dedication that far exceeds the majority of new traders. It is that same level of dedication that success requires. I spent years struggling to find success as a trader. I was fortunate enough to have the ability to tread water in the market until I learned. I survived until I thrived. It did not come naturally to me, and I had to overcome emotional roadblocks about the fear of loss that so many traders experience. I learned through the long process of trial and error. I hope I am able to help save you the pain of that process by showing you the strategies I use every day. This book is a compilation of my years trading in the markets. I have traded through the turmoil of 1000 point market crashes and experienced the pure excitement of 1000% biotech short squeezes. Over my years trading, one of the biggest things I have learned is to never underestimate the market.

Every trader is a hunter of volume and volatility, and a manager of risk. Every new day in the market presents a new set of challenges and opportunities for growth. The market is dynamic and no two days are ever the same. I have had days where I made tens of thousands of dollars, and I have had days where in a matter of minutes, I gave back three months of profits. The life of a trader is one of ups and downs. Trading is a career that certainly will not bore you, but could overwhelm you if you are not able to cope with the emotional pressures. I emphasize to all of our students, the importance of balance in life. The best traders learn and maintain techniques to cope with stress, and remember to take time to get away from the computer screens and enjoy life. We work hard and we play hard. This is the life of a day trader. I hope you will join us.